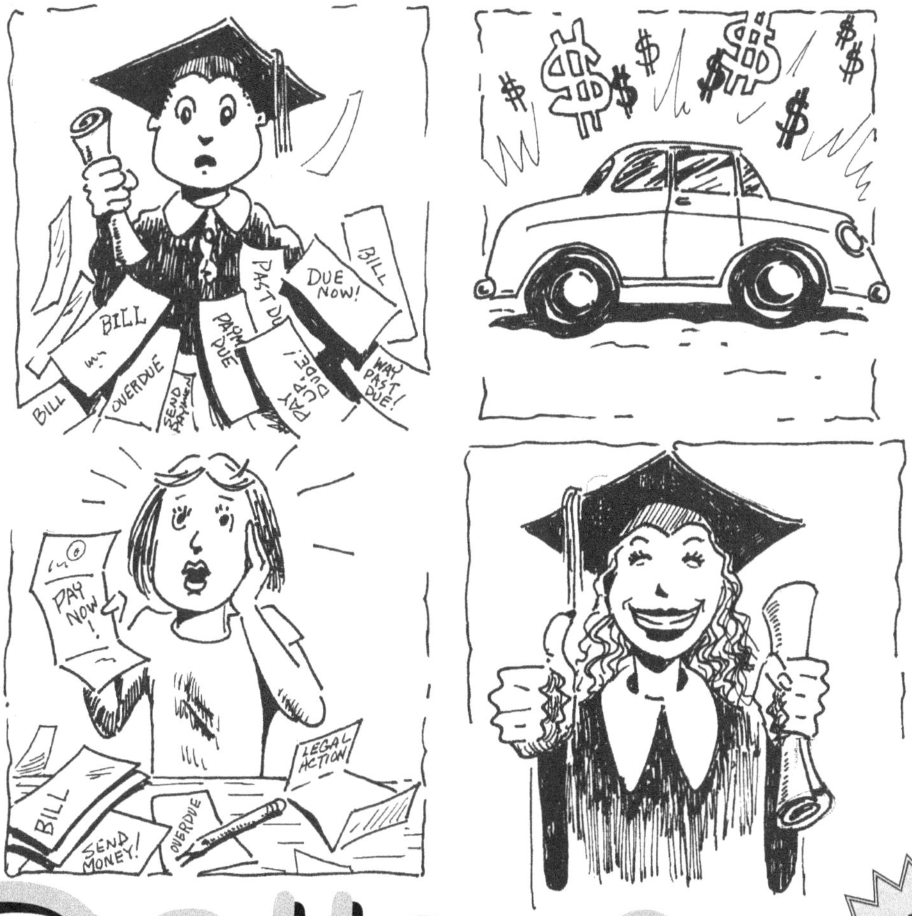

Dollars & $ense

2nd Edition – Sensible Strategic Concepts for Life

A Guide to Financial Security

By Sherry Raines & William Austin

NEW FORUMS
Stillwater, Oklahoma
U.S.A.

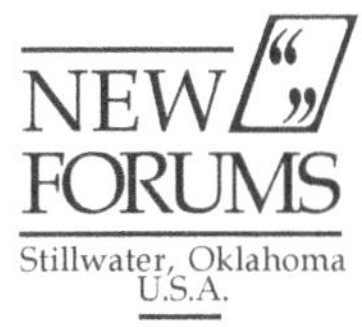

NEW FORUMS PRESS INC.

Published in the United States of America
by New Forums Press, Inc.1018 S. Lewis St.
Stillwater, OK 74074
www.newforums.com

Library of Congress Cataloging-in-Publication Data Pending

This book may be ordered in bulk quantities at discount from New Forums Press, Inc., P.O. Box 876, Stillwater, OK 74076 [Federal I.D. No. 73 1123239]. Printed in the United States of America.

ISBN 10: 1-58107-156-6
ISBN 13: 978-1-581071-56-6

Cover and Inside Art by Robby McMurtry.

Second paperback edition / 2 3 4 5 6 7 8 9 0

Sherry Raines Dedication

to
Dan, Jason and Emily

for your encouragement, love and support.

William Austin Dedication

for
William, Miranda & Tristan

May your financial futures be bright and provide you with happiness.

Professional Endorsements

Sherry Raines has provided a simple, practical guide to every day financial information that can be used by students at all levels. This basic information is invaluable and can really help students manage their finances as they begin the transition to life as independent adults. Definitely required reading for all students!

Connie Duffy, Vice President, Human Resources,
Horiba Jobin Yvon, Inc.

Sherry's commitment to helping young people have the best possible financial start in life is relentless. This resource highlights the critical information needed to successfully manage the complex financial choices they will face in their near future. As a professional and a mother she brings a unique and easy to understand perspective to these important issues. Bravo!

Kimberly Martinez, President, Bonitas International

In the fifteen years I've known Sherry, I have always found her to be driven and to succeed at all she attempts, whether that be mentoring a high-potential employee, teaching a financial education class, or making a presentation at a business meeting. She has a real interest in helping others to succeed and a knack for transferring knowledge so that the learning process is effortless. Her goal is always to help people so that they can grow and help themselves. It's been a pleasure to call Sherry first a colleague, then my financial planner, but always a friend for these many years.

Gregory Wells, Vice President, Learning and Development,

Table of Contents

Sherry Raines Acknowledgements

For as long as I can remember, I have always wanted to write a book. I always imagined it would be a child's book or a representation of some life experience. Interestingly, this book is somewhat a blend of both these concepts. I have tried to "write a story" for teens and young adults so they can learn how to handle their money effectively and become financially responsible.

Working in the financial services industry for over twenty-five years has given me an extensive background in both the technical and practical aspects of this "business". While many financial professionals have focused on wealth management for affluent clients, I have chosen to apply my knowledge to the financial education of those who are just starting their financial journey. With education and proper guidance I hope they will be able to enjoy the lifestyle they choose and achieve the financial independence they desire.

Meeting Dr. Will Austin was a pivotal point in my career. Will has a remarkable ability to identify new opportunities and to turn concept into reality. I truly believe that without his input and direction, the project would not have gotten this far. He understands and shares my vision of the importance of financial literacy in our children's future, Will continues to enrich the experience for the students at Warren County Community College by raising the standards and pioneering new educational opportunities.

Over the years I have had the privilege to work with several people who have contributed to my personal development and ultimately to the completion of this book. I would like to thank Howard Nager, Leslie Gaber, Judy Goldstein, Gregory Wells, Margie Feather, Kimberly Harrington, Connie Duffy, Denise McCue, Judy Yellin, and Maryann McIntosh for being my rooting section, my cheerleaders, and for helping me believe that I am as "capable" as they think I am.

Dick Nolan has been a great teacher and mentor. Aside from being one of the most knowledgeable professionals in the financial services industry I have ever met, he has shown me that ethical, caring individuals in this business make a difference every day in the lives of others. I would also like to thank Barry Horowitz for his technical advice on chapter 4. Barry is an exceptionally talented Tax Advisor and unselfishly gave up his valuable time during "tax season" to see this project through. Chapter 9, Basics of Insurance, was carefully reviewed and edited by Dick Hogarth, who is absolutely the most talented and effective "Group Insurance" executive around today and his comments were invaluable.

I would like to thank Rhona and Neil Stein for their excitement and encouragement. I think they were the very first people I told about my plans for this book. They are an incredible support system and provided exceptional business advice and guidance that has helped me tremendously. I would also like to thank my parents, Beverly and Joseph for instilling the work ethic that has enabled me to succeed in all that I endeavor.

Many people have added to the success and development of this book, but I would like to acknowledge the contribution made by three people in particular. My husband Dan, who aside from being my "IT" guy, is my constant source of encouragement; my daughter Emily who thinks "I can do anything" and has helped cook many meals while I worked and my son Jason. Jason is my sounding board, my eyes and ears into the college "scene" and is my right hand man. Thank you!

William Austin Acknowledgements

This work represents the realization of over a decade of work in the field of higher education research. In 1997, I conducted my first survey of non-returning students attempting to address retention in higher education. I realized from the data that a very high percentage of community college students would stop-out, not transfer, and not obtain a degree. The organizational manager in me suspected that this would be due to poor experiences by students with the institutions were I worked. In my first study, which my friend Craig Jacobs termed "Project Lazarus," I determined that the most frequent reasons students failed to persist through to graduation had very little to do with the institution and more to do with "personal issues." Over the course of ten years, I have refined and conducted the Lazarus study several more times, learning that 80% of "personal issues" were really "personal financial issues." I learned that students are interrupting their college careers because they cannot adequately manage their personal financial affairs.

I must thank Dr. Robert Messina, President of Burlington County College (NJ) for hiring me into my first research position and allowing me the autonomy and freedom to work toward improving retention at his college. I must also thank, Dr. Peter Contini for hiring me at Salem Community College into my first research management position and for providing me the funds to conduct the second version of "Project Lazarus."

While at Salem, in 1999, I first began to work to address these issues with the assistance of Ron and Dori Ingersoll of the Enrollment Management Center in Tampa Florida. They were instrumental in enlightening me beyond research and problem identification toward creating solutions for problems, ultimately ensuring that more students would be successful. It was my early work with them in engaging students in financial planning that led to my interest in developing this work.

Over the next six years, I would make many attempts at developing a work product to address this problem in higher education. It was not until I met Sherry Raines that I finally found the person as passionate and most equipped to operationalize student financial planning into a lifelong journey of personal financial management. Her financial expertise and passion for the subject matter are the foundations for this work. Thank you also to Stephanie Tettemer for introducing me to Sherry.

I would also like to make some personal acknowledgements to people who made the completion of this book possible. I would like to thank the Warren County Community College Board of Trustees (Edward Smith (Chair), Gladys Blemmer, David Boone, Harry Brown, Terry Clancy, Craig Dana, Dr. Terrence Finnegan, William King, Holly Mackey, Annette Munley, Betti Singh, and former Trustees Scott Churchill, Cindy Dorio, John McCann, Jack Sweet, Erwin Naumann & Steven B. Van Campen) for giving me the freedom in my contract to author and publish works of non-fiction. I would like to thank Barbara Pratt, JoAnn Schaible (Chapter #4), Sharon Hintz (Chapter #8) & Jessica Leeper (Chapter #6) for all their expertise, advice and attention to detail in assisting me with the editing of this book. I would like to thank Daria Kissenberth for her wonderful graphic design work and for her attention to detail in creating a sample chapter for publishers. I offer special thanks to Doug Dollar and New Forums Press for having the faith to publish my work for a second time.

Finally, I want to thank my wife Lori for all her efforts and support in creating this work. I also want to thank my children William, Miranda, and Tristan who continue to forgive me for all the times I was late getting home, or absent from a game, or too exhausted to play.

1

Your Financial Lifeline

Notes:

...money influences a baby's future.

Welcome to the beginning of your financial success!

Money and how you handle it will be an essential part of every stage of your life. Even as a baby, money was incorporated into decisions that were made about you and your future. Money provides you with shelter, food, education, transportation, better health, access to opportunities, and supplies you with greater autonomy to pursue happiness. It is very important for you to be aware of how to properly manage and control your money.

As young adults, most college students already have plenty of experience with money - some good, some bad. Most of us love having it and want more of it. Money can be a great motivator. In fact, most people attend college because it can lead to better career options, which in turn often means more money.

In order to maximize your financial potential, you will have to learn how to handle monetary situations at every life stage. So let's start at the very beginning:

First answer the following questions:

1. My parents never talked about money in front of me Yes____No ____
2. My parents taught me about money and how it works Yes___No____
3. My family never had enough money True___ False____
4. My family always had enough money True___ False ___
5. The most important thing to me about money is_________
   ____
   ____
6. The income that would place me into the top 5% of all earners in the United States is $________________________. (Hint: answer can be found at www.census.gov).
7. The yearly income I need to make to support my lifestyle is $___________.
8. The amount of money I need in my savings account to feel comfortable is $__________________.
9. The amount of money I want to have for my retirement is $__________________.
10. The amount of money I would like to donate to charity every year is $__________________.

Using the answers to questions 5-10, close your eyes and create a visual picture of your life five years from today. Based on your visual image of yourself, are you managing your financial situation well enough now to realize that vision?

How you answer these questions will have a significant impact on your spending habits throughout your life.

From the moment we are born, our financial life begins. It is important to make ourselves knowledgeable about what accounts we may or may not have so that we can monitor and manage them properly as we grow.

Sometimes relatives and friends send monetary baby gifts:

Check Off Those That Apply To You

- ❒ Savings bonds
- ❒ Cash gifts (includes checks)
- ❒ Stocks
- ❒ Mutual funds
- ❒ Life insurance

Do You Know Where Your Money Is?

Sometimes these gifts are placed in the child's name in what's called a Uniform Gifts To Minors Account (UGTMA) and it is co-owned by the parent or guardian until the child becomes of legal age to own the account outright. This age varies by state and is usually 18 or 21. Talk with a financial professional to find out the age in your state.

Sometimes the money is held for the child in the parent's name. The ownership of the account determines how taxes are paid and may influence the ability of the child to qualify for educational financial aid. This can be a complicated topic and should be discussed with your financial advisor or accountant.

...money from the tooth fairy.

Forming Healthy Attitudes

During childhood, our financial education begins as we come into contact with money and begin to understand that it does not grow on trees. We begin to start accumulating money from the tooth fairy, allowance, birthdays, and holidays.

Our personal philosophy on dealing with money begins to develop during childhood: some children will save indefinitely only making small purchases here and there while others become "big spenders" dropping all their money on the latest toy. Your parents and their spending styles may have influenced many of your spending habits. **Check off which of the following applied to you:**

...dropping money on the latest toy.

- ❒ I never received allowance
- ❒ My tooth fairy left change
- ❒ My tooth fairy left bills
- ❒ I spent whatever cash gifts I received
- ❒ I saved my money gifts
- ❒ I saved some, spent some
- ❒ My parents always had the latest gadgets
- ❒ We discussed money and its management in our home
- ❒ My parents never discussed money

Most teenagers have jobs and if they don't, they should. We start to have adult money issues at this time because we have cars and like to go out with our friends. Suddenly, you have to think about things like taxes, checking accounts, saving accounts, understanding a paycheck, benefits, insurance, expenses and wait a minute... COLLEGE!

There will always be many more things to spend our money on than means of earning money. That is why it is important, especially during your teenage years to learn to manage money properly and get the most out of it.

List all expenses you have or had as a teenager:

1. ____
2. ____
3. ____
4. ____
5. ____

Notes:

Getting Started

Interestingly enough, when you get your first job and start earning an income, this is best time to learn how to:

1. Read a paycheck
2. Understand company benefits and deductions
3. Learn the facts about taxes
4. Begin a small retirement savings plan.... yes you read right!
5. Cashflow management
6. Debt and Credit management
7. Balancing a checkbook
8. Budgeting
9. Investing
10. Insurance basics

Sounds like a lot to learn? You bet, but the truth is, teenagers are faced with real adult issues once they begin to earn money, spend it and become responsible for their own financial needs. The earlier you learn the basics, the more money you will have later on in life.

If you choose to spend your paycheck on movies, dates, IPODs, video games, etc., you will soon learn how to spend every dollar you make. You will learn to purchase items that give immediate gratification. You will **not** learn how to build wealth, how to manage money for the long term, how to invest, or how to ensure a financial future that leads to happiness.

...how I will pay for college?

One of the biggest concerns for most students is to figure out how they are going to pay for college. Before you can figure this out, you have to choose the right college. This is one of those early financial decisions in your life that requires thinking carefully about the pros and cons of the choice you make and how you and your parents will be affected. The choice you make can impact other aspects of your life (and your parent's lives) for a very long time.

So, how will you pay for college?

- ❐ Scholarship
- ❐ Parents pay for it all (ha! ha!)
- ❐ Parents and/or students pay for it out of savings or income
- ❐ Parents and or students take loans
- ❐ Work your way through college
- ❐ Combination of the above

Usually it is the combination that works but not always. And don't forget, many occupations today require graduate education as well.

Now let's take a look at how much college may cost you:

Annual Cost: $25,000 for a four-year Private College (Room and Board included)
Average Inflation rate 5% (times each previous year amount)

Example:
Year 1, $25,000
Year 2 $26,250
Year 3 $27,562
Year 4 $28,940
Total for 4 years $107,752 Wow!

Note: Cost and aid figures are from the College Board's *Trends in College Pricing 2008, Trends in Student Aid 2008,* and *Education Pays 2007.*

Check with local financial aid professionals and guidance counselors for the different loans available to you and your

Notes:

parents. Remember to investigate a number of scholarship options. You and your parents pay taxes to support these professionals at public institutions near your home; it is their responsibility to guide and assist you.

Please don't buy into the old adage that the college that charges the most will provide you with the best education. Recent studies have demonstrated that elite universities only provide graduates with an early advantage for about five years. It is your work competency and productivity at the workplace and in life that will make a difference in your income and success throughout life. Plus, that early advantage may be negated if you are making 30 years of student loan payments.

Other Pressing College Issues

In addition to paying for college tuition and board, you will have to consider the following:

- ❒ Money for going out
- ❒ Spring break or holiday retreats
- ❒ Car payments and gas
- ❒ Housing and living expenses (dependent on your circumstances)
- ❒ Clothing and purchases
- ❒ Books and various learning materials

...consider money for relaxation.

How do you pay for these now? Credit cards? See chapter 7 to learn more about managing credit and how it will impact you financially.

So you have finished college, got a dream job and decided to give your folks a break and move out of the house. What do you do next?

Where You Live

Most graduates will rent an apartment and some may consider buying a condo or house. Can you buy a house or condo or do you have to rent? If you can afford it (complete a budget worksheet and talk to a real estate broker) you may want to buy. It can be a good investment and every time you pay your monthly payment you are paying yourself, not throwing out money. However, not everyone can afford it so you may have to rent, especially when you first start out. Some other things to consider:

- ✔ Real Estate market conditions may not be right for buying at all times.
- ✔ If you plan to live in a place for less than three years, you should consider renting. The costs involved with buying may not justify the investment.
- ✔ Coming up with $10,000 or $25,000 for a down payment may not be possible at this early stage.

✔ Owning a home usually includes other expenses like property taxes, home maintenance and upkeep that may be too costly right now.

The Car You Drive

If you live and work in a city, maybe you should forgo the car and take public transportation. It saves you a lot of money and is often a "pain in the neck" and potentially very expensive to park.

If you're like most young adults, you want and need to have a car. So therefore, what do you do, buy or lease? If you can, you should buy. Eventually, the payment will be done and you will actually OWN something. It will be an asset, no longer a liability and you may be able to go without a loan for a while and save the money you were paying each month. When you lease, you will have to keep making payments indefinitely. The payments are never done and roughly every two to three years you will need to make another down payment. Also, if you need or prefer to drive a lot, the lease option is probably not for you as you will have to pay for all the extra miles that you put on the odometer at the end of the lease.

...consider financial choices.

Of course, you can drive a "fancier" car normally with a lease, but you do not have pride of ownership. Here is where your answers to those questions about where you want to be in five years will become very important.

Time to Reflect

Describe again how you see your life after college or in the next five years. Did you make any changes after considering all the details about money you need to be mindful of throughout life? By creating a mental picture now, it will help you make the financial decisions along the way that will help you achieve your goals.

____

Notes:

The remainder of this book will help to clarify some of the ideas and examples of this chapter. However, each person's goals will differ as well as each person's story and life experiences. The best means to wealth is in the realization of your personal plan for financial success, not in comparing yourself to others. Realizing your vision is the only method of achieving happiness. Concentrate on your vision, build a life to realize it, and manage your money in conjunction with that vision and you will master money and wealth.

2

Your Net Worth: The Resources You Begin With

Notes:

Starting With a Strategy

Remember the game "Pin the Tail on the Donkey" that you played as a child? You were blindfolded and spun around several times before you were let get go and pushed off to take your turn. You staggered in a dizzy state, doing your best but did not realize where you were going and ended up sticking that tail everywhere but where it actually belonged!

That is great fun for a child, but as you get older, building your financial strategy should not be approached blindfolded or thought of as a game. The sad reality is that most people today still approach their finances in a state of dizzy blindness, spending or saving money without clear direction and focus. That's another way of saying they don't have a process or strategy to achieve their financial goals.

In the previous chapter we talked about creating a vision of your financial goals and how you can best achieve them. One thing we already know is that if you are still reading this book, you want to have money and create wealth. How much you need to accumulate is up to you, but one thing is certain, you must have a way to monitor and measure your ***Net Worth*** along the way.

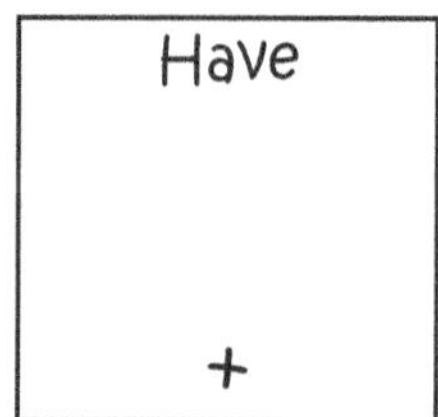

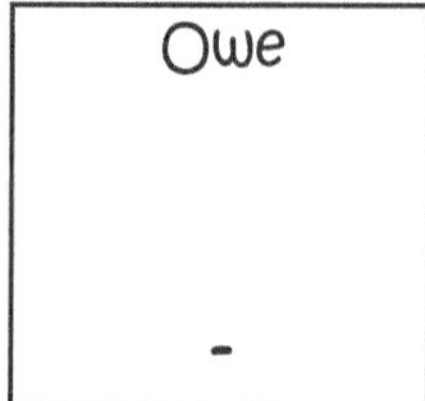

Understanding Your Net Worth

On the left side of the scale, write the amount of money you think you have, on the right side of the scale, write the amount of money you think you might owe. Which way would the scale tip for you? Draw an arrow in the direction the scale will tip for you. Learning how to manage your money when you are young will give you a head start and may help to tip your money scale towards the positive side instead of the negative one.

Fortunately, a lot of people are given a head start by friends and relatives. As young children, they may receive savings bonds, or have savings accounts created in their names. By having knowledge of these accounts, and continuing to manage them properly, you set yourself up for a positive financial future and a greater ***net worth***.

That brings us to the term ***net worth***. What exactly is it and what is it used for?

Assets	• car
	• boat
	• cash in bank
Liabilities	• apartment rent
	• car loan balance
	______________
Net Worth $______________	

Your **net worth** is the sum of your assets minus your liabilities. **Assets** include all the things that you have like your money, your savings, whatever you own that has value such as a car, a house, jewelry, etc. Your **liabilities** are what you owe including student loans, car loans, credit card debt, etc.

Your net worth tells a story about you. It shows how well you save, how much you spend and how close or far you are from achieving your financial goals. Before a bank will be willing to give you a loan for a house, or a car, or for school; they want to know how much money you have. It is in their business interest to determine what type of risk you might present.

... your net worth tells a story about you.

You want to make sure that your net worth is growing over time, and that the ratio of debt to assets moves towards assets and away from debt. If a bank thinks that you have too much debt and not enough assets, you might not be able to afford the things that you want to buy later in life. It will be more difficult to get a loan if you have too much debt.

Banks and financial institutions like to use a worksheet called a **Net Worth Statement** to determine if you are financially responsible, and a good risk to lend money to. The Net Worth Statement on the following page is an example of a very basic one.

Fill it in with your current information. Always show the date so you have a reference point and can look back for a comparison. It is important to remember that there are no right or wrong answers when filling out your net worth statement. It is not a competition or grade report, but rather a stepping block from which you can improve upon. Your goal should be to constantly and continuously improve and increase your net worth. Also, remember that this statement is for you to use, fill it in accurately, filling it in to what you would like to have can be done as a second step, but your baseline is a reality you want to face and realize.

...tip the scale in your favor.

Notes:

...banks look at your net worth.

Net Worth Statement

Date____________

ASSETS

Cash Equivalents

- ❒ Checking ________
- ❒ Savings ________
- ❒ Money Market ________
- ❒ Certificates of Deposit ________
- ❒ Cash Value Life Insurance ________

Investments

- ❒ Stocks ________
- ❒ Bonds ________
- ❒ Mutual Funds ________
- ❒ Other Investments ________

Retirement Funds

- ❒ Traditional IRA ________
- ❒ Roth IRA ________
- ❒ 401k or 403b ________
- ❒ Lump Sum Cash Balance ________

Personal Assets

- ❒ Home ________
- ❒ Car ________
- ❒ Jewelry ________
- ❒ Collectibles ________
- ❒ Other ________

Total Assets ________

LIABILITIES

- ❒ Credit Card Balance ________
- ❒ Student Loans ________
- ❒ Car Loans ________
- ❒ Mortgages ________
- ❒ Personal Loan ________
- ❒ 401K Loan ________
- ❒ Home Equity Loan ________
- ❒ Other ________

Total Liabilities ________

Net Worth (Assets minus Liabilities) ________

The net worth worksheet has three possible results.

- ❒ Assets = Liabilities
- ❒ Assets greater than Liabilities = **Surplus** (money leftover)
- ❒ Liabilities greater than Assets = **Deficit** (owe money, debt)

Which one are you today? Which one do you want to be?

...loser

...winner

You will want to create an accurate picture of your current financial situation and revisit it periodically. Whatever your personal outcome is, don't fret; the net worth statement is not a static document. It changes as your life circumstances change. With effort and proper planning on your part, you can increase your assets and have them far exceed your liabilities. Your net worth statement should be reviewed annually or whenever there is a significant change in your life, monetary or personal, such as a job, marriage, or baby.

As you review your net worth statement, also review your goals, desires and needs. Perhaps your outlook on the type of lifestyle you want to support will change over time, resulting in your needing more or less assets. Or maybe the condition of your net worth will drive the change in your objectives. Whatever you decide to do, you will be well equipped by understanding your financial status through the use of the net worth statement.

Time to Reflect

As you begin to consider your net worth, think about the goals you are setting for your life. Do you want to live a middle class life of comfort? Or are you slightly more daring, and want to take a little more from what life has to offer? To reach the higher plateaus that our society has to offer, you will need to contemplate your worth very seriously, to consider what you want it to be in the future, and to begin to make the minor changes now that will affect your future.

Perhaps you need to rethink your career choices to ensure you make the income you desire; perhaps you need to sacrifice now, spending less to accumulate more wealth that you can then build upon. Financially successful people follow independent paths. They don't follow people, buying without thinking, growing their debt and hoping for the best. They set goals, they work hard to reach those goals, and they celebrate and enjoy a life that they have envisioned. Now is the point in your life when it will be easiest to break away from the pack, to strike off

Notes:

...your cash assets must support your lifestyle.

in an independent direction not only toward financial security but also toward financial success.

Net worth is important, but so are your cash assets. You can have a positive net worth, but still have a financial problem. For example, you could live in a million dollar home and not have enough cash to pay the mortgage or to furnish it. In the United States today there are thousands of empty "McMansions," inhabited by people living paycheck to paycheck. Therefore, it is also essential that you learn to live within a budget.

3

Budget? What's a Budget?

Notes:

Budgets...

This is your "Facts of Life" chapter. If you thought your first "Facts of Life" discussion with your parents was awkward, just try asking them about their financial situation or retirement plans. Most people don't like to talk about money and parents most certainly do not want to discuss personal money issues with their children. In addition to their natural discomfort, many parents do not have the skills and knowledge to have this discussion with their children. Frankly, they probably never learned it themselves.

In case you're wondering what this is all about, it's called MANAGING YOUR MONEY and being FINANCIALLY RESPONSIBLE! Most people go through life working, spending money, paying bills, playing and eventually, if they get to it, they might actually start saving and investing money. The problem is, the saving and investing money is always the last thing people do with their money and they rarely have anything left to save.

The only way you will have money to use for those major life goals is to learn to budget. Budgeting is used for everything from time management to sports competition to managing money. Learning how to budget your money is one of the most important skills you will ever learn. It all starts with figuring out the difference between WANTING something and NEEDING something.

What is the difference between a WANT and a NEED:

WANT: A want is something you desire having because of the benefits you feel you will enjoy or incur by owning it. It is not something you **must have** in order to function or meet basic daily life issues. It is a form of self-gratification, which can be good, but in excess will cause sleepless nights and stress if your wants exceed your means.

NEED: A need is something you are required to have in order to maintain basic life requirements.

Examples: You **need** a car to get to work
You **want** a Maserati instead of a Chevrolet

You **need** to make your car payment
You **want** to take a trip to Mexico instead of making your car payment

You **need** to have a morning coffee (this need is a stretch)
You **want** to have a $4.00 latte instead of a cup of homemade coffee

You **need** a basic phone to ensure effective communication
You **want** a fancy mobile phone, with text messaging, video, GIS, and MP3 capabilities

You **need** clothes to stay warm and stay within legal and moral restraints
You **want** new clothes to look great and stay in style

The choices you make on how you spend your money each day on every purchase will ultimately determine how you will continue to live your life and make financial decisions.

If you always go with the want instead of the need, you will be less likely to build the financial future you desire. If you choose immediate gratification over long term stability and success you will miss out on a great life where you have real freedom.

Let's go through an exercise to see how you are managing your financial decision making today.

These two columns will help you identify how many of the things you spend money on are for wants or for needs. List 5 to 10 things you spend money on every month and put it in the column you think it fits in.

WANT	NEED
1.__________	1.__________
2.__________	2.__________
3.__________	3.__________
4.__________	4 __________
5.__________	5.__________
6.__________	6 __________
7.__________	7 __________
8.__________	8 __________
9.__________	9 __________
10.__________	10.__________

Notes:

If you find that you have more wants than needs and spend most of your money on those, then there are few things you will have to consider.

1. Can you afford them or are you buying them on credit?
2. Do you really need them or do you just want them?
3. Does having them make you really happy or are you happy at the time of purchase and later indifferent to your things?
4. Do you need to get a different or second job to make more money?
5. Are you only working to pay for the extra stuff?
6. What if you took some of the money you spent on wants and saved or invested it instead?
7. Is there even a single want you can do without so you might save some money?

Now that you understand how spending money on wants versus needs affects your ability to meet your overall goals, you are now ready to learn how to create a financial budget and use it to build the kind of life you want to have.

...creating a budget.

Creating A Budget

A budget is a worksheet that is similar to the **Net Worth Statement** we worked on in Chapter 2. Only the budget focuses on your **cash flow**, how much money you earn each month and how much you spend. The bottom line will show you if you are spending too much, have any money left to save or invest and whether your expenses are for wants or needs.

Income:

List all the sources of income you have each month. This is before you have anything taken out for taxes, expenses or savings. This would include allowance, money you earn on a job and investment income. This income is known as your gross income and is the salary your employer will use to offer you a job.

Taxes:

Yes, you have to pay taxes. Out of the income you make each month, you have to pay taxes to a number of governmental agencies including: the federal government, state government, sometimes local government, Medicare, unemployment, Social Security and possibly more.

Expenses:

This is where life and financial budgeting start to get interesting. You have different types of expenses. Some are fixed, the same amount each month like rent and car payments. Some are variable expenses that change each month such as food, phone bills, credit card bills.

Insurance:

So you think you don't need to pay for insurance? Guess again. In a later chapter we will briefly review the different kinds of insurance but for now, let's focus on car insurance, health insurance and possibly renter insurance.

Savings:

If you already have money that you are saving each month, good for you! This is the section you will have to do the most work on. Learn how to pay yourself first to save or invest and then use the rest to pay your expenses.

Total Expenses:

This is the section that adds up all the money that comes out of your checking/savings each month. This is the sum of all your expenditures.

Surplus/Deficit:

If your disbursements are less than your income then you have a surplus, money left each month. If you spend more than you make, you have what is called a deficit and this may lead to debt. To determine this figure, subtract your total disbursements from your net income - is the number positive or negative?

Turn to the next page to begin work on your BUDGET.

Notes:

Cash Flow Analysis – Budget Worksheet

	Current Monthly	*What It Should Be*
Income		
Allowance	______	______
Job	______	______
Total Income	______	______
Fixed Expenses		
Rent/Mortgage	______	______
Car Loan	______	______
Property Tax	______	______
Student Loan	______	______
Variable Expenses		
Food	______	______
Telephone(s)	______	______
Gas/Tolls/Parking	______	______
Car Maintenance	______	______
Personal Care	______	______
Entertainment	______	______
Utilities	______	______
Cable/Internet	______	______
Charities	______	______
Clubs/Memberships	______	______
Credit Card Bills	______	______
Insurance		
Car Insurance	______	______
Renter Insurance	______	______
Health Insurance	______	______
Life Insurance	______	______
Disability Insurance	______	______
Taxes		
Federal	______	______
State/Local	______	______
Social Security	______	______
Medicare	______	______
State Unemployment	______	______
Other	______	______
Savings		
401K/IRA	______	______
Savings	______	______
Mutual Funds	______	______
Other	______	______
Total Expenses	______	______
SURPLUS or DEFICIT	______	______

And the Answer Is ...

Quite an eye-opening experience isn't it! No one ever realizes how much money they actually spend unless they take the time to do the budget worksheet. Now, do you have a surplus or a deficit?

If you have a deficit, what can you do to change that to a surplus?

1. Spend less money
2. Make more money
3. Reduce taxes

Remember, the quickest way to become wealthy is to make more money while simultaneously spending less.

...an eye-opening experience.

Spend Less Money

List some ways you can spend less money. Look at your budget and see which expenses you can cut back. Highlight them. Remember, this is the time you may have to decide if your expenses are wants or needs. Even if they are needs, can you spend less on them?

Things I do not really need:

1. ______________________________
2. ______________________________
3. ______________________________
4. ______________________________
5. ______________________________

Make More Money

To make more money, maybe you need to get a better job, a second job or both! This may be the time to start thinking about your career choices and whether or not you will be able to earn the kind of money you will need to support the lifestyle choices you make. Here is a great time to research what types of employment will help you increase your means.

- ❒ Do you have the right skills for a better job?
- ❒ Do you have the right education?
- ❒ Do you have the drive, ambition, and appropriate attitude to take more from what life has to offer?

Notes:

Reduce Taxes

Another method of increasing savings capability is to cut the amount you are required to pay in taxes. Reducing taxes can sometimes be very simple but more often than not, the one area that is difficult to change. Are you getting money back each year when you file your income tax or do you end up paying? Perhaps you need to talk to an accountant about the number of exemptions you take. You may also need to consider opening an IRA (to be discussed later) to save money and get a tax deduction. Participating in your employer's 401k or 403b plan will do the same.

...see more choices for your future!

Perhaps you already have a monthly surplus (more money left than you spend). Does that mean you should you spend more? NO! It means you should do the same exercise as above so you can have even more money left. THEN, you should SAVE or INVEST it!

We'll talk more about saving/investing later on in this book. For now, think about starting a high interest money market account and if your company has one, make sure you are contributing at least the minimum to your company retirement plan.

Smart Money Tips

If you have any loans, pay them down and off completely. See chapter 7 about credit cards. Systematically pay them off and each month put money away to save for the future. Before you know it, you will have eliminated all debt and accumulated a very nice sum of money to use for important life needs such as paying off school loans, buying a condo or house, getting married, buying a car, taking a vacation and saving for retirement.

So what would you rather do, spend extra on "those wasteful wants", run out of money each month and never save OR, watch what you spend, keep your expenses down, maximize your earnings, save for the future and have more choices for your future? You decide!

Most of all do not let anyone stop you, diminish your dreams, or listen to people who tell you success is not all its cut out to be, they are failures already.

Earning Money & Paying Taxes

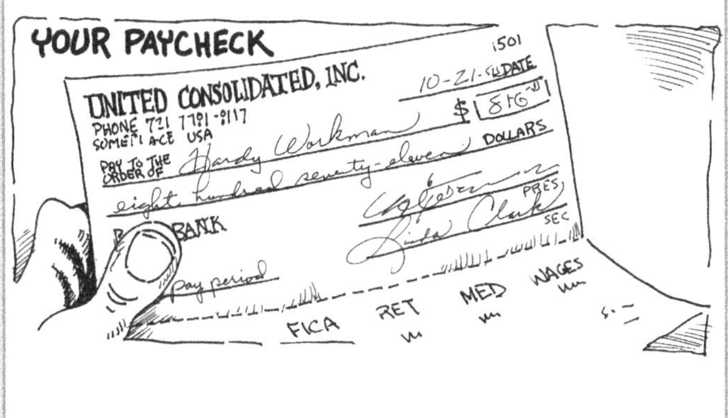

Notes:

Taxes

In this chapter we will review earning money and paying taxes. These are two of the biggest responsibilities working individuals face. Instead of assuming you understand what they are about, we are going to take an entire chapter to explain each of these and tell you what you need to know about each of them. Although a full book could be devoted to each of these topics, the basics are important to know to get started on reaching your financial future. Remember it is always a good idea to talk to a tax professional if you have more questions about your taxes.

The Infamous W-4 (See the Appendix for a sample.)

Let's start at the very beginning of the tax process. Most likely, you are either working now or plan to at some time in the near future. Whenever you start a new job, you will have to fill out forms to begin the payroll process. One of these forms will be called the "W-4." This is the form that determines your filing status for tax purposes. That means how many exemptions you claim and your marital status. If you are in high school or college, it is likely you are going to select single, with one or zero exemptions. Let's leave it at that for now. We will explain it further when we talk about taxes later on in this chapter.

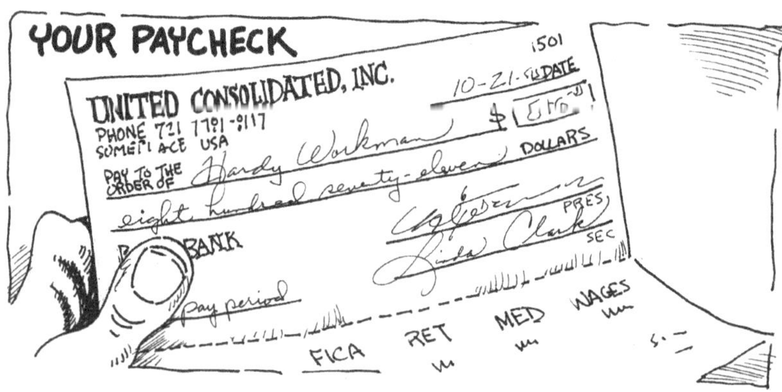

...beginning of the tax process, prior to your first check.

Unless you are doing volunteer work, you will receive a regular paycheck with a paystub when you work (with the exception of those who are self-employed or work on commission). Understanding how to read a paystub and the various elements that make it up are very important. It may seem very simplistic but many people after years of working still don't know how to read their paystub. This is important because you need to know if the correct deductions are being made, if the amount you are receiving is correct and if the employer is reporting everything correctly. Many people run into problems when they complete a W-4 incorrectly and then have inappropriate deductions taken out.

The key sections of your paystub are:

1. Name and address
2. Social Security number
3. Gross and Net payments
4. Pay rate
5. Pay Period
6. Number of hours worked
7. Overtime payments
8. Exemptions and Tax Status

9. Benefits signed up for and deducted for
10. Vacation time accumulated

Get Out Your Paycheck

As we go over each section, check off the box once you have reviewed this section on your paycheck and have made sure it is accurate.

First things first, make sure the name and address on the check is from the company that employs you. Many employers use payroll companies to process their payroll and they do this for many employers. Make sure you are receiving it from the employer you work for and make sure you get one from each company that employs you if you have more than one job. (See page 26 for an illustration of an earnings statement keyed to the points below.)

1. Name and Address

Make sure your name is spelled correctly and they have your most current address so that all important documents are sent to you at the correct address. If you move, make sure your employer is informed so they can change their records and yours.

2. Social Security Number

This must be correct and agrees to your Social Security card. All tax information utilizes this number. If you want to be credited for the taxes you paid, they must have the right social security number. NOT ALL EMPLOYERS display this on the paycheck due to privacy issues and identity theft concerns. Make sure your employer has your correct number in their records if you cannot see it on your check. Remember, it is not impossible for a company clerk to misstype your number into their payroll system. Your Social Security number is the most important identifying factor that is issued to you during your lifetime and will never change.

3. Pay Rate

Your pay rate is the amount you are getting paid either hourly, weekly, monthly or annually. Usually it is an hourly rate even if you get paid on an annual basis. This doesn't change often but when you get a raise or promotion you should make sure it is changed to coincide with the date of your salary change. If you are paid hourly, you need to make sure that the correct amount is paid for all days that you work. Sometimes you will receive different pay rates for different days and schedules, (i.e.) more on weekends and holidays.

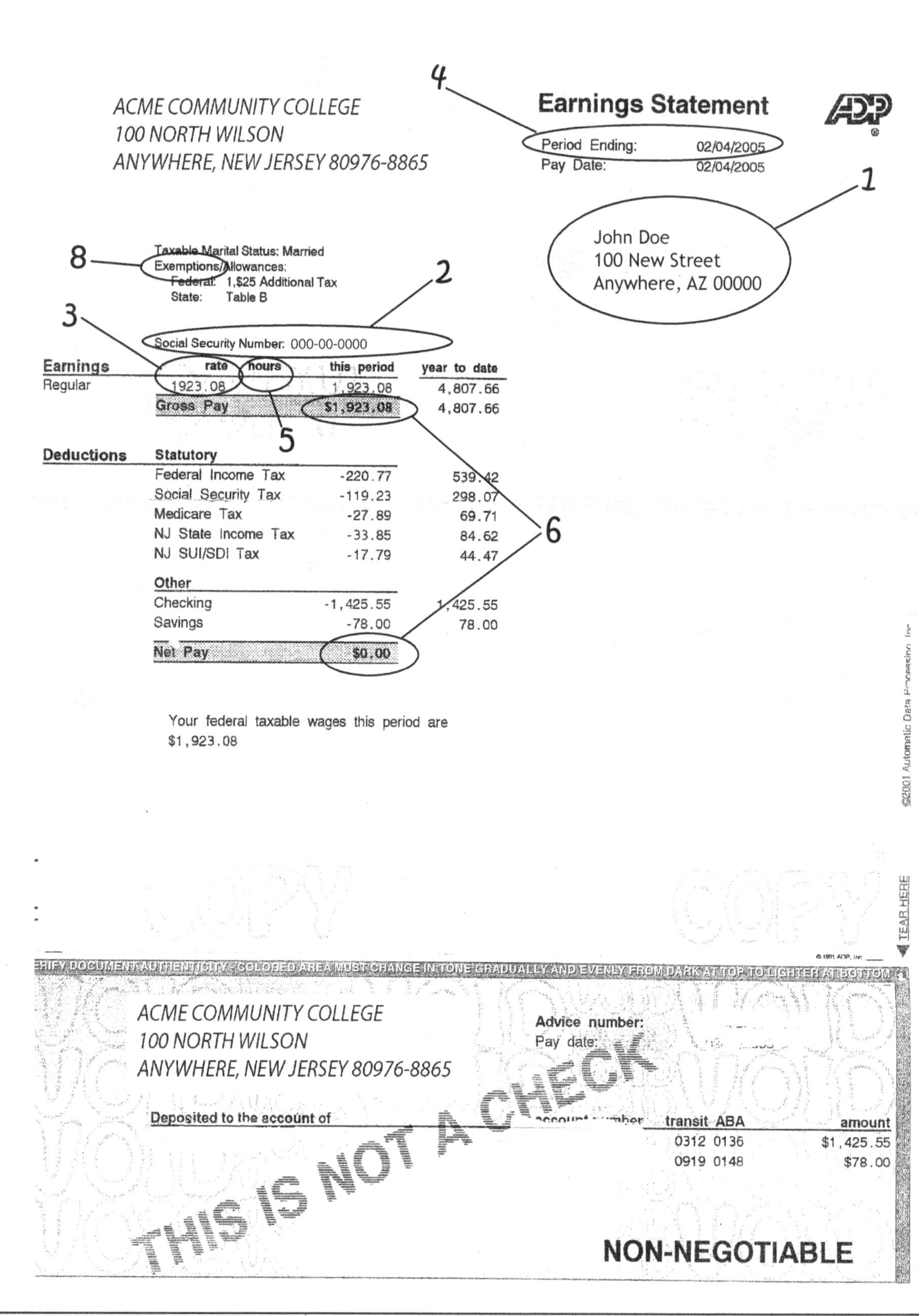
ACME COMMUNITY COLLEGE
100 NORTH WILSON
ANYWHERE, NEW JERSEY 80976-8865

Earnings Statement

Period Ending: 02/04/2005
Pay Date: 02/04/2005

John Doe
100 New Street
Anywhere, AZ 00000

Taxable Marital Status: Married
Exemptions/Allowances:
Federal: 1,$25 Additional Tax
State: Table B

Social Security Number: 000-00-0000

Earnings	rate	hours	this period	year to date
Regular	1923.08		1,923.08	4,807.66
Gross Pay			$1,923.08	4,807.66

Deductions	Statutory	this period	year to date
	Federal Income Tax	-220.77	539.42
	Social Security Tax	-119.23	298.07
	Medicare Tax	-27.89	69.71
	NJ State Income Tax	-33.85	84.62
	NJ SUI/SDI Tax	-17.79	44.47
	Other		
	Checking	-1,425.55	1,425.55
	Savings	-78.00	78.00
	Net Pay	$0.00	

Your federal taxable wages this period are $1,923.08

ACME COMMUNITY COLLEGE
100 NORTH WILSON
ANYWHERE, NEW JERSEY 80976-8865

Advice number:
Pay date:

Deposited to the account of

account number	transit ABA	amount
	0312 0136	$1,425.55
	0919 0148	$78.00

NON-NEGOTIABLE

4. Pay Period

Each paycheck is for a specific period of time. It is either a weekly, biweekly (every other week) twice a month (15th and 30th) or monthly paycheck. Sometimes, you will receive a paycheck out of cycle that is used to pay for overtime or a bonus. You must check the dates of the check and the hours and rate you are being paid for so they are correct. You need to make it a habit to regularly examine, verify, and correct your paycheck. Mistakes do happen and rarely are they in your favor, and even if they are the company may be entitled to a refund later (regardless of the origin of the error).

5. Number of Hours Worked

If your employer uses a time clock to monitor your hours worked, this section will always be different. It is unlikely that you will always come and go at the exact same time. However, those minutes that you come in late or leave early mean less money in your pocket. Remember that when you are trying to come up with a few extra dollars for coffee or gas money. More importantly and contrary to popular opinion, those people who only give it half an effort do not reach the top.

It's a good idea to keep a record of which dates and how many hours you worked. This way, if you ever think your employer didn't pay you the right amount, you can check your own records.

6. Gross and Net Payments

Gross Payment is the amount you receive **before** any deductions are taken. This is usually the hourly rate times the number of hours you work. It may include overtime or bonus money. Net Payment is the final amount you receive **after** all deductions are made. This includes taxes withheld from your paycheck, loans you may be paying back to your employer, savings, and benefit deductions. The Net Payment is the amount you will see in your check or the amount deposited in your bank account (if you have direct deposit). It is always important to understand the differences between gross and net pay and become comfortable with this terminology.

7. Overtime Payments

When you work overtime, if you are an hourly employee, you must check and see that you are being paid for the correct number of hours and at the correct pay rate. Sometimes people are paid a higher rate for certain hours or days. Make sure this is accurate. You should also make sure that all deductions are being taken out of overtime payments so that you are up-to-date on all payments that you owe for taxes or savings plans.

8. Exemptions

This is the number you selected on the W-4 Form. It determines how much is taken out of each paycheck for taxes.

Notes:

Before Tax and After Tax

The taxes you pay are based on your gross salary. Your gross salary is the entire amount you make before any deductions are taken out. When you pay for benefits such as medical insurance with **before tax dollars**, the deductions are taken off the gross salary and then the taxes withheld are calculated on the reduced salary amount. This usually results in less taxes being paid and more money for you. This is a smart way to help reduce your taxes and keep more of your income in your pocket.

After tax deductions are taken off your salary after taxes have been calculated and subtracted and then the payment for the benefit or deduction comes off. This does not give you any tax advantage. It may however, sometimes increase the benefit you receive. For now pay as many of your deductions as possible with **before tax** dollars.

Exemptions and Tax Status

This is where you determine how much taxes are taken out of your paycheck and are reported to the federal, state and local governments. It should be a relatively simple action but is often more complicated. The government tax forms have calculation worksheets to help you figure out the correct amount of taxes to withhold. This should theoretically result in the correct amount of taxes withheld. Sometimes, you may owe or receive a refund when you file your tax return.

If you are single and have only yourself to declare, then you would indicate single, one. If you find you end up owing more money to the government when you file your taxes, you may want to have more money withheld. If you end up getting money back, then you might want to adjust your exemptions and have less money withheld so you have more to use during the year. See a tax specialist for the appropriate advice in your circumstance.

Some people think that you should have as little tax withheld as possible. This can be complicated and you should talk to a tax professional to help figure this out. **For now, if you are single and have no dependents, just go with single, one exemption.** The U.S. Government is not as forgiving as your mother, and it is wiser to pay what is owed so you never have to face any fines and/or penalties.

Benefits

If you are fortunate enough to work for an employer that offers benefits, you should take advantage of them. Generally, part time employees are not eligible for as many, if any benefits, at all. These benefits are worth MONEY and when you participate, they can save you money, give you money or protect you from unexpected financial obligations. In fact, smart employers consider benefits part of the total cost of employing you. When you compare multiple employment offers you should consider benefits as well as salary in job offer comparisons. These benefits will be discussed in more detail in a later chapter. Just make sure that your paycheck indicates both your correct benefits and/or deductions that you had elected. Occasionally, employers do make mistakes and you are not enrolled in the benefits you thought you were so the proper deductions may not be taken out of your pay.

Vacation Time

Some employers help you keep track of how much vacation time you have earned and used up on your paycheck. Once again, you should keep a personal record of all the time you have taken off and why you were off. Was it for sick time, personal time, vacation time or travel for work? Keeping track will help make sure you are paid properly and are able to take off as much time as you think you are entitled to use. Some employers will pay you at the end of the year for vacation time you do not use. Each situation is different and should be both negotiated and analyzed when considering your total compensation.

Direct Deposit

Let's take a moment to talk about direct deposit. Very often employers will give you the option of being paid by direct deposit. This means the employer will electronically send your net salary to the bank account of your choice, either your checking or savings account. You have to elect this option and provide your personal bank information. **Direct deposit is worth considering** because it generally gets the money into your account before you could get there yourself to deposit it. It also prevents you from cashing the entire check and spending it all before you use it for important things like paying your bills! It also helps prevent your check from getting lost or stolen. So, in most cases, go with direct deposit. Some people like the feeling of getting the actual paycheck and cashing it right away. DON'T DO IT! It's not cost effective and its antiquated. You receive no benefit from opting out of direct deposit.

If you do elect direct deposit, you will still receive a pay stub or pay invoice, the part of your payment that lists all the deductions. Please continue to look at it every time and make sure it is accurate!

Payroll Taxes

Congratulations! You now know how to read your paycheck and paystub. We talked about the various sections of your paycheck but did you notice the one section we DID NOT discuss? In case you missed it, we're talking about the TAXES withheld. You already know that your Gross Salary will have deductions taken out. Taxes account for the greatest deductions in your paycheck. They include the following taxes:

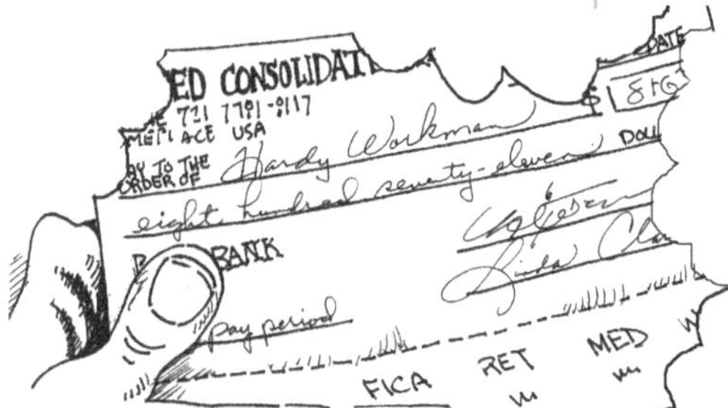

... your salary will have deductions taken out.

Notes:

- ❐ Federal Taxes
- ❐ Social Security (FICA)
- ❐ State, Local and possible Wage Taxes
- ❐ Medicare
- ❐ Unemployment and/or Disability Insurance Taxes

In most cases, the employee (you) are required to pay all these taxes. The employer takes them out of your salary and reports them to the various governmental agencies. Here are some basic facts you should understand about each of these taxes.

Federal Taxes

There are tax tables that determine which tax bracket you fall into. The more money you make, the higher your tax bracket, the more money comes out of your paycheck to go to the Federal government. Speak to your tax professional for more information on your tax bracket. There are ways to reduce your tax bracket even as your income increases, including:

- ✔ Before-tax deductions for certain benefits
- ✔ Saving through your company's 401K or 403b or IRA
- ✔ Changing your filing status

These are all ways to reduce your tax bracket.

Social Security (FICA) and Medicare

FICA stands for Federal Insurance Contributions Act. This tax is what the government uses to pay retired citizens their social security retirement benefit. It also provides basic income benefits to widows, disabled citizens who qualify for benefits, and children who have lost working parents. See the web site www.SocialSecurity.gov for additional information on this topic.

The Social Security tax is one of the few taxes that are paid by both the employee (you) and the employer. Each one pays a set percentage of the salary up to a maximum amount.

Once the maximum is reached, your employer will stop deducting it from your paycheck. Quite often, the maximums increase and they are so high now, that fewer people are reaching that maximum and continue to pay these taxes throughout the year.

Medicare

This is a tax that currently is a set percentage and is unlimited. Medicare taxes are used to pay for basic social services some citizens require support for. Some of these include: medical care and hospitalization. This percentage changes periodically and is likely to go up, as the government needs more money for welfare programs.

State and Local Taxes

All taxes are used to support different governmental agencies. Federal taxes you pay go to the Federal Government for federally supported programs such as welfare programs like Medicaid, Federal highways, for defense spending, and a myriad of other Federal programs. State taxes are paid to the state government for things the state is responsible for such as transportation, human services, colleges and universities, etc. Each state has different tax rates. You pay state taxes to the state you work or live in and the rules for this vary by state.

Local taxes are sometimes imposed when you live in a city such as New York City or Philadelphia where additional taxes are required. You may pay a local wage tax that goes to support schools, transportation, or other needs that it is determined that you may be using while working.

Generally, when you live in one state and work in another, you only pay state taxes on your earned income in the state where you are employed. For example, if you live in NJ and work in NY, then you would only pay state income tax for NY. You still may have to pay to your home state for other taxes. Keep this in mind when job searching.

State Unemployment and Disability Insurance Taxes (SUI or SDI)

State unemployment tax (SUI) is paid by both the employee and the employer, and the employer pays the higher amount. This tax is intended to help provide temporary income support for employees who lose their job. It usually lasts a limited time period and you must prove that you are actively job searching.

...what, I lost my job!

When you do qualify, you receive unemployment benefits after you fill out the proper paperwork and go through the bureaucratic process. The amount you receive is a percentage of your salary up to a maximum.

People do lose their jobs! This might happen because of poor job performance (yes, your fault) or when the employer makes changes and decides to eliminate jobs. If your job is eliminated or the employer fires you for reasons that are not due to things you have done to cause it, you may be eligible for unemployment insurance. The key thing to remember here is

Notes:

that YOU MAY NOT QUALIFY for unemployment benefits JUST BECAUSE YOU LOSE YOUR JOB! If you quit your job because you do not like it you will find it more difficult to collect on unemployment insurance as the employer will likely fight your application.

State Disability Income Tax (SDI). Several states also have separate disability insurance that is sometimes paid by the employer and sometimes paid by the employee. If this tax is paid, then the employee is eligible for short-term disability income benefits if they become disabled. Short-term disability benefits assume that the employee will return to work within a limited time such as six months. The benefits only last for approximately six months after which the employee may apply for long term Social Security Disability benefits. The benefit amount for short-term disability benefits is similar to the amount an employee may receive if they received unemployment benefits. It is a limited amount not intended to replace the full income. State laws vary so make sure you check with your employer on this.

Taxes, Taxes and More Taxes.........

So how much do all these taxes add up to? No need to guess, check off all the taxes that apply in your state and fill in the appropriate taxes that come out of your paycheck:

- ❒ Federal Tax ___________
- ❒ State Tax ___________
- ❒ Local Tax ___________
- ❒ Medicare ___________
- ❒ Social Security (FICA) _________
- ❒ Unemployment Tax ___________
- ❒ State Disability Tax ___________

Your Total Taxes ___________

Now you know why it is important to make sure you are selecting the proper exemptions, filing status and utilizing your before-tax deductions. The good news is that you are not alone. All responsible adults who are employed pay these taxes. The best thing that you can do is become educated about how to minimize the taxes you pay by employing as many smart tax strategies possible.

People often become upset about taxes. One way to sleep better at night is to consider an old European saying:

> *"Taxes are merely the bill we pay to live in a civilized society. The cost of anarchy, chaos, and civil war is far more than the cost of taxes."*

5

Basic Financial Decisions — True Dollars & Sense

Notes:

Making Sense of It All

Whatever your current financial issues, there are basic principles that you can use to make better financial decisions. Each of us must learn to employ a 'Dollars and Sense' lifestyle because we must learn to use common sense to make financial decisions. It is not always about saving the most money or spending the least (although it is a good basic principle). Sometimes it is about spending less now so you have more down the road.

Many financial decisions require thinking about what makes the most sense for you later on and how decisions you make now will help or prevent you from reaching your financial goals. Each decision can affect you throughout your life, so let's get started.

Consider some of the big money issues you face as a young adult?

- ❒ Getting a job
- ❒ Going to college
- ❒ Buying a car
- ❒ Renting an apartment
- ❒ Buying a home (house or condo)
- ❒ Taking vacations
- ❒ Dating
- ❒ Getting engaged
- ❒ Getting married

Basic Principle #1

Get a job!

Financially responsible people get a job when they are able to start working. THIS DOES NOT MEAN YOU MUST WORK A 40-HOUR WEEK! Even a part-time job will help. What are the benefits from working?

- ❒ You earn money to pay for the things you **need** and, yes, **want** to have.
- ❒ You can begin saving money for future purchases.
- ❒ You develop skills that can be used in the future.
- ❒ You meet new people, some will be friends, some will be contacts for future jobs (this is very important).
- ❒ You develop credentials for your resume.
- ❒ You begin paying taxes and making purchases creating a credit history.
- ❒ You learn to make your own decisions and to develop financial independence.
- ❒ You determine what skills and job functions you like or don't like .
- ❒ You realize if further education is needed to get the type of job you really want.

- ❒ You realize how hard you have to work to make money and maybe you spend it more carefully.
- ❒ You become a financially responsible adult.

Most people do not stay with the same job forever. You are likely to change jobs, if not careers, a minimum of 5 to 7 times over your professional career. Each job helps you prepare for the next one and each change you make should help you attain a different level of satisfaction. What are some reasons people change jobs?

- ❒ Make more money
- ❒ Get a promotion
- ❒ Change careers
- ❒ Develop new skills
- ❒ Move to a new location
- ❒ Work fewer hours
- ❒ Do something they really love
- ❒ Retire
- ❒ Adventure
- ❒ Meet new people
- ❒ Start a business

Starting a business is a great idea. Not all people are able to do this nor do they want to. If you have the desire and the concept, go for it. Keep in mind that many new businesses fail but some succeed. There are many resources available to help you.

Principle #2

Get an Education

Most young people go to college today. There are a number of ways to become educated and college is just one of them. However, as stated before, it is a fact that most college graduates get higher paying jobs with better benefits than people who do not go to college. Does that mean you have to go to college right after high school? The answer is not necessarily. Let's analyze how different approaches may impact you (see table to the right).

You may be convinced now that going to college is the right choice for you. Now you have to figure out which one to go to and how to pay for it. Think about the costs and benefits of the choice you make.

College Approach	Positives	Negatives
Two-Year College After High School		
Four -Year College After High School		
Armed Forces after High School, College later on		
Full-Time Job wait to go to College		
Part-time Job and College part-time		
Part-time Job and College full-time		

Notes:

Which college should you attend?

This is a difficult topic. Many people choose a college based on name or reputation. Others select one based on location, close to home or far from home. Others choose based on courses of study and others select because of affordability. Whatever the reason, you have to give this serious thought. It is a tremendous time and cost commitment and should not be taken lightly. There are many resources available to you to help you decide such as:

- ❐ High School Guidance Counselors
- ❐ College Student Assistance
- ❐ Web sites specific to college selection (use a search engine to find one)
- ❐ Career Counselors (check with community organizations)

Key points to remember:

- ❐ You can be happy with any decision you make as long as you make the best of the situation
- ❐ Utilize all the resources available to you at the college you select and you will do well
- ❐ Apply yourself and get involved. Make your college your community and build relationships there.

How will you pay for college? (Check all that apply.)

- ❐ Parents pay for all or part of it
- ❐ Student loans
- ❐ Work my way through college
- ❐ Work/study where you work and go to school at the same time to help pay
- ❐ Employer offers tuition reimbursement
- ❐ Combination of the above

When your parents pay for your college education you should realize the financial impact it will have on them. Unless they are affluent and have managed to save the money needed or can afford to pay for it out of pocket, they will need to make changes in their financial situation to pay for it. This is a big commitment on their part so make sure you make the most of your experience to get your or their money's worth!

It may make sense for you take student loans even if your parents are paying because you may get better rates and payment schedules than they can get. Then, they can pay the loans for you, or like many of us you may learn a valuable lesson in paying for them yourself.

Principle #3

Spend Your Money Wisely

The major money issues you face always involve spending money, making purchases that cost a lot of money and financing some of your purchases. This section will try to give you some basic rules to follow that should help you make smarter *short term* decisions that will have better *long term* outcomes.

Cars............

The big question is always whether to **buy** or **lease** a car. In most cases, you should buy instead of leasing. When you buy, eventually you will be done with payments and actually own an asset. True, the asset will be depreciating (losing value) but you could always sell it, trade it in or just continue driving it for awhile and save the money you would have otherwise been using for car payments. When you lease, you always have a payment and never have an asset that you own.

...always the big question.

Then why do some people lease? Sometimes you want a vehicle that is very expensive and you cannot afford to purchase it. The only way you can afford to have it is if you lease it. Why is that? Because when you lease a vehicle, you only make payments on a part or percentage of the vehicle.

Payments on the leased vehicle are lower because instead of financing the full value of the car, you are only financing half or less than half of the value of the vehicle. Sounds like a good deal until you realize that you've paid to use the car for 3 or 4 years and then you have nothing to show for it plus you have to start all over with a new lease. If you were paying off a purchase, at least at the end, you actually "own" something and no longer have to make more payments.

So maybe the real question is, what type of vehicle should you get? Answer some of the following questions to help you decide:

1. Do you really **need** a new or different car or do you just **want** one?
2. Can you afford to make the payments without wrecking your monthly cash flow?
3. How much **should** you be paying monthly so that you can **afford** it?
4. Is it necessary to have a car that costs more than you can afford?
5. Can you be satisfied with having a car that is less expensive or status oriented?

...big shot or more cash?

Notes:

These are the dollar and sense questions, the needs versus the wants. Cars are just a means of transportation; they do not really indicate success or status. Anyone can own an expensive vehicle if they are willing to make the lease payments. Only financially responsible adults select vehicles based on sound decisions that don't jeopardize their financial futures.

There is another option that may allow you to have the best of both worlds, low price and ownership along with the prestige of the car you desire. Look for high end used car purchases of an expired lease. For instance, the car of your dreams may be more affordable for purchase if you buy it after someone else has leased it for a 24-month period.

Other Basic Principles to Live By

Housing

When you look for a place to live, location is critical. It should be close enough to where you work to minimize transportation costs but it should also be affordable, no more than 25% of your gross monthly income. When you can afford to, consider purchasing a condo, townhouse or small home. The tax benefits or investment may be a very important early financial decision.

Vacations

Taking a vacation is important to your mental health. How often you take vacations and where you go, what you do on them is another story. Sometimes, just taking time off and doing activities locally can be adequate. It's not always necessary to take a big trip that lasts only a week and costs a few thousand dollars. This will be a big purchase to pay off. Consider the benefits before you take the plunge!

Dating

Dating may be necessary to meet the partner of your dreams. It can also be expensive. If your potential partner cannot save money, needs to live an extravagant life that he/she cannot afford, consider how your life may end up. Be careful, pick someone that is sensible and will make a great life partner.

Marriage

Getting married. Be sure your partner and yourself share the same financial goals and have shared with each other financial objectives. The day you get married, one half of everything you used to own gets a new co-owner, your spouse. Romantic love is a wonderful adventure, but many divorces are often traced back to financial problems.

Smart Tip

Saving even just a little money each month will eventually make a tremendous difference in your financial stability. Think about this ...

> If you save $25 a month and earn even a very conservative 5% interest on it, reinvest all the earnings and do this until you are 50 years old (assume you are 20 now), you will have accumulated over $20,000. Just imagine if you increase this amount every year.
>
> Hopefully what you have learned in this chapter is that you have to use the needs and wants analysis, the dollar and sense logic. Is the purchase something that will give you immediate gratification or will it have long-term value.

Notes:

6

Financing Education/Loans

Notes:

College

Going to college has many benefits in terms of developing new skills, meeting people, great adventures and life lessons. It helps prepare you for adulthood and ultimately, leads you to a fulfilling career. Sounds good doesn't it? It is but unfortunately, there is a price you may have to pay. How much you pay and how much debt you incur is up to you.

Choosing Your Future Level of Debt

We've already determined that you determine your future level of debt based on when and where you go to college. There are a few questions you need to consider before you can approach financing your education. Which of these categories do you fit in?

1. Who is paying for college?

- ❒ My parents are paying and have all the money already saved.
- ❒ My parents are paying but they do not have enough saved.
- ❒ I am paying for college myself with money I have saved up.
- ❒ I am paying for college myself but don't have enough saved.
- ❒ My parents and I are sharing the cost of college.
- ❒ I am getting a partial scholarship.
- ❒ I am getting a "full ride" scholarship.

2. Have you made a decision regarding what you would like to study?

- ❒ Yes, I know what I want to major in and what career I want.
- ❒ No, I have no clue.
- ❒ Not sure.

3. What are the most important aspects to you of your college experience?

- ❒ Status and name recognition of school.
- ❒ Attending school in a certain city or region.
- ❒ Having fun, get serious about a job after.
- ❒ Obtaining best education and getting job offers.
- ❒ Becoming an educated person.
- ❒ Opening a new world of possibilities and social networks.
- ❒ Limiting expenses.
- ❒ Completing a degree and going on to graduate school.
- ❒ Finding a spouse or partner.

Hopefully you've given these types of questions some careful consideration before you selected the college you are going to attend. We could spend an entire book debating the issues but we won't. After answering these questions, you decide how much you are willing to pay or ask your parents to pay so you can have the college experience of your choice.

College Payment Techniques

When most people think about paying for college, they think they either have to pay for it from savings or take loans.

If you are going to college, you will need to complete a financial aid form (FASFA) that is required by the Federal government. Even if you do not qualify for grant funds (money you do not have to pay back), you will need to complete this form to be eligible for Federal loans, many scholarships, and many types of internal institutional aid. We will talk more about this later on.

...FAFSA is a must!

Some tips on the financial aid form:

1. File as early as possible. Some states have established priority deadlines for state aid. In other cases, the institution may have some funds available on a 'first come, first served' basis.
2. If you are a dependent student, your parents will also need to fill out this form and it will take their tax records to complete it. This means your parents should be trying to complete their taxes as early in the annual process as allowed by law.
3. Do not panic if the college asks you to provide additional information. Approximately 1/3 of all students receive this request annually. However, it does mean you need to have your forms and taxes completed earlier as you will have to wait out this bureaucratic process.
4. File for financial aid each year, especially if something changes (e.g., you have a sibling who also begins to attend college or a job change happens to you, or your parents that influences total family income).

The financial aid process is designed to determine your "**expected family contribution**," known as your **EFC** - this is the amount both you and your parents are expected by the Federal government to contribute to your college education. **Here is the secret many people do not realize.** Your EFC is exactly the same whether you want to attend an expensive Ivy League Institution, a public college, or your local community college. Your EFC is based on your family's circumstances - the maximum amount you can reasonably be expected to pay for college. The total amount of aid you will be eligible for is the difference between the total cost of the college you would like to attend and your EFC.

TOTAL COST - EFC = YOUR FINANCIAL AID ELIGIBILITY

Notes:

So, if your total cost of attendance (Tuition, Fees, Room & Board, etc.) is $35,000 and your FASFA outcomes demonstrate through the EFC that you can only contribute $12,000 per year, then you will be eligible for $23,000 in financial aid.

However, before you think all your college payment problems are solved and you get ready for that big check, remember that there is a limited amount of money provided by grants. So, if you go to a higher priced college your financial aid may be made up of the maximum amount in loans for you and your parents. Institutions often give you an internal grant or scholarship (i.e., they just cut their tuition for you) to make up the difference. In many cases these price cuts will only take place after they have exhausted their ability to leverage public grants and loans to cover your tuition. Examine every offer of financial aid carefully, what may appear wonderful at first may really be a sophisticated sales technique that is really not in your favor in the long run.

Conversely, if you go to a lower priced institution, more of your costs may actually be covered by grants and/or scholarships. This is money that you will not have to repay with interest later in life.

Fortunately, there ARE other ways to pay for college.

- ❒ Work while you go to school and pay for it as you earn
- ❒ Employer tuition reimbursement
- ❒ Put off going to college and work first
- ❒ Military scholarship

...list sources of money.

Tuition reimbursement is by far a favorite. Some employers will help pay for your college education. Generally, you enroll in a degree program, take courses and when you pass with a certain grade, they reimburse your costs. Sometimes they require that the courses and degree are job related. Sometimes they don't. If this option fits into your lifestyle choice, go for it!

Let's go through this step-by-step:

Step One

List the sources of money available to you:

Some of the sources are:

- ❒ Money already saved
- ❒ Scholarships
- ❒ Financial Aid (grants and loans)

Find out what savings are available to you from all sources.

Make a list of all sources of money that was saved for you since childhood. The following types of savings you might have and not know about:

Source	Amount	Owner-ship	Rate of Return	Rank Of Use
Passbook Savings				
Certificates of Deposit				
Savings Bonds, Bonds				
Mutual Funds				
Stocks				
529 Plans				
Coverdell Education Savings Accounts (CESA)				
Trusts				
TOTAL AMOUNT SAVED				

Source

Savings accounts and Certificates of Deposit are usually held in banks, some people use on-line or internet sites now as well. Savings Bonds and Bonds are usually purchased through banks or institutions and are usually kept in secure locations like safe deposit boxes. Mutual funds and stocks are purchased through investment companies or banks and may be purchased over the web too. Coverdell and 529 plans are special savings/ investment plans that invest the money that are usually sold by banks and investment companies. Trusts are more complicated legal methods used by some people to transfer ownership of money to manage taxes and to save money for college.

Ownership

Once you have identified all the savings, **find out who has access to the money!**

WHAT? That's right, **some accounts may not be in your name** or you cannot access them without someone else signing for it. Sometimes the account is held jointly with another person called a UTMA account (Unified Transfer to Minors Act). You can only access these accounts by yourself once you are 21 (or the legal age in your state).

...some accounts may not be in your name.

Rate of Return

Fixed Rates of Return are based on interest rates. This is a pre-determined rate that stays the same. It is usually fairly low (less than 3%) and has minimal risk of losing money. Even if interest rates go down, you will not lose any of the original investment amount, you will just get a lower interest rate on the money saved.

Notes:

Variable Rates of Return mean the rate does **not** stay the same. It can go up or down and the rates are usually dependent on the stock and/or bond markets or economic conditions. Because of ongoing market volatility, performance may be subject to substantial changes. They are at more risk than fixed rates because if the rates go down, you can lose some of the original amount you invest. However, the upside is that they can grow at a higher rate than fixed investments and over the last several decades, the average annual rate of return of the stock market has been over 10%.

Rank of Use

The major considerations here are:

- ❐ Which account to take from first
- ❐ Reviewing the investments to limit your risk
- ❐ Consider tax implications
- ❐ Analyze investment returns on stocks

Generally, you should take money from the lowest rate of return account first (which is generally your fixed investments). This gives the variable accounts more time to grow. **One word of caution,** this is the time to talk to your financial professional about the variable accounts and make sure they are invested appropriately to limit the risk of these investments. You will need the money within a 5-year time frame and may want to reconsider the loss potential if you are not willing to see a reduction in the value of the accounts.

You also need to consider the nasty T word … TAXES. Some of the accounts that have been growing Tax Deferred (you don't pay tax on the money you earn until you take out the money) might result in taxation of the gains (the amount you earned on your investment) and could affect your income tax return.

Stocks should be considered carefully to determine if you will make money or lose money, if there are dividends and what your tax liability is. It's confusing and you should discuss this with a professional prior to making any changes.

Total Amount Available

Now you have a good idea how much money you have already accumulated for college. But it may not be enough. So where else can you get money?

EXPENSES	AMOUNTS
Tuition	
Fees	
Room and Board	
Transportation	
Other	
Total Expenses	
SOURCES	
Scholarships	
Savings	
Total Sources	
Amount still needed to Finance	

After you've completed this table, you have determined that you still need to finance some or all of your education. You and/ or your parents can borrow money from a number of sources. If you decide that loans are the way to go, here are a few to consider:

Step Two

Who Should Borrow, Students or Parents?

- In some cases, it may make more sense for the loan to be in your name. Some loans are only available to students and they may have better terms (loan rate, repayment time) than loans available to parents. If that is the case, then the student can take out the loan while parents can still help make the payments.

- Sometimes parents may not be able to make the full payments but can help pay the interest on the loans while you are in school. This will greatly reduce the total amount you will have to pay at the end, notably if you only qualify for unsubsidized loans.

- Establishing a credit rating is a good thing. Taking out a loan in your own name and making payments on time will go a long way towards establishing a strong credit rating. Don't forget the reverse is true, if you miss payments, are late or simply don't pay them, you will hurt your credit rating which can have serious consequences later on.

Notes:

Step Three

What loans are available?

You MUST complete the **FAFSA (Free Application For Federal Student Aid)** forms. They are submitted to **CSS (The College Scholarship Service)**. Most of you already submitted this when you applied to college. Even if you don't expect to get any scholarships or grants (money you don't have to pay back), you still need to send in the FAFSA to see how much you will be offered in terms of subsidized and unsubsidized loans, work-study programs or other types of aid.

Before we go on, you need to understand the difference between subsidized and unsubsidized loans. Generally, subsidized loans are need-based (meaning you qualify based on financial standards). Subsidized loans are always the better deal.

Subsidized:

- ✔ The Federal Government pays the interest due while you are in school.
- ✔ Repayment of the loan is deferred until 6 months after graduation!!!

Unsubsidized:

- ✔ Interest payments are required while you are in school or add the interest on to the total loan.
- ✔ Repayment of the loan is still deferred until 6 months after graduation, but interest accrues.

Some loans are available to students and others are available to parents. There are certain things you need to consider before you sign on the dotted line for a loan:

1. Don't borrow more than you need! The temptation is great but remember, you will have to pay it back eventually.
2. Student loans generally make more sense economically than parent loans so try to get as much money from these as possible.
3. Make sure you consider that you may have to pay fees for the money you borrow. Look for loans with the lowest fees. You may end up with less money than you think after you pay the fees.
4. Don't wait until the last minute to apply. You may not receive the money in time to pay your bills.
5. Find out the different payment options the schools offer to see which one fits best with your financial situation. Maybe paying monthly will allow you to borrow less and pay more as you go along. You won't know until you sit down and figure it out.

Loans available to Students

1. **Stafford Loans**
   Allows undergraduate and graduate students to borrow on either a subsidized or unsubsidized basis. The maximum amounts available per year vary based on the following:
   i. Year of college (freshman, sophomore, etc.)
   ii. College vs. Graduate school
   iii. Dependent vs. independent student (still lives with parent or guardian)
   Check www.salliemae.com for current limits and other pertinent information.

2. **Perkins Loans**
   These are loans available to students based on financial need. They have fairly low interest rates and do not have to be paid back until after you finish school. Note: not all colleges offer these loans.

3. **PLUS Loans**
   These are loans available to your parents. They generally have higher interest rates than Stafford or Perkins loans. Payments must begin after 60 days of receiving the loan. So if your parents take a loan out in August, they have to start paying it back in October. They can generally take out larger loan amounts than you might qualify for from the Stafford or Perkins loans if they are not enough.

4. **Private Loans**
   These are loans that you or your parents take out on your own, through credit unions, banks, workplace etc. Conditions vary and generally they have the highest interest rates. Please do a lot of research before you decide to pursue private loans.

   There are qualification requirements for all the loans, so make sure you review them early and carefully. Check www.salliemae.com for more information.

Step Four

Repayment Options

CONGRATULATIONS GRADUATE!

Exciting times! Celebrations! Partying! Moving! Traveling! Marriage! New Jobs! And...............................BILLS!

How do you make sense of all the bills and how do you pay them?

...the bills are a part of graduation.

...forgot some of your loans?

Notes:

Where do you start?

- ❒ Do you know what all of your loans are and how much they are? Sometimes people do forget. But you need to find out so if you're not sure, you can check the
  - National Student Loan Data System at http://www.nslds.ed.gov/
  - National Student Clearinghouse loan locator at www.studentclearinghouse.org
  - Your college financial aid office may also have information on file for you.

- ❒ Read all materials provided to you about your loan. You will receive important information from lenders on when you must begin to make payments or any changes about your payments. Laws may change while you are in college or during your repayment period. It is your responsibility to stay informed about these changes.

- ❒ Make a list. Fill out this table below

Loan	Amount	Interest Rate	Due Date	Term of Loan
Subsidized Loan				
Unsubsidized Loan				
Car Loan				
Credit Card				
Mortgage				

- ❒ Pay at least the minimum payments on all loans except subsidized loans that you don't have to start paying for 6 months. DO NOT MISS A PAYMENT!

- ❒ Pay the highest amount you can afford on the loans with the highest interest rates.

- ❒ As you pay off one loan, increase payments on the loan with the next highest interest rate.

- ❒ There are some rare opportunities to have some part of your loan canceled. Extreme disabilities, certain types of volunteer work and/or military service can qualify for what's called payment forgiveness. You will have to check with the lender to see if you qualify.

- ❒ Getting a deferment where you delay paying back the loan is a little easier but again, you need to check with your specific lender to see if you meet the conditions. **Even during a deferment, the interest will continue to add up** so you may want to at least **make the minimum**

interest payments. Remember, you're just delaying the date to which you have to start paying back the loan amount, **it will not go away completely!**

- ❐ Consider consolidating your loans. The loans you have are likely to have variable interest rates. That means they go up or down based on the Treasury bill index. Every year, your interest rate will change and there will be times when the rate can be quite high. Keep an eye on interest rates and when we are in a low interest rate market, you may want to consolidate the loans into one fixed rate loan for a designated period of time.

Another word about taxes:

Don't forget that you may be able to deduct some of the interest on the taxes that you are paying on the loans. This is dependent on your income level and if you are single or married. Check with your financial professional or tax preparer.

Tax Credits

There are two tax credits available to those students who qualify.

The Hope Scholarship Credit

Currently up to $1500 of eligible expenses are available as tax credits as long as the student goes to school at least half time. It is only available for the first two years of post-secondary education. You must meet certain income requirements. You must be a dependent on your parent's tax return.

The Lifetime Learning Credit

This credit gives you up to $2,000 of tax credits per family (not per person) and is also dependent on income. Unlike the Hope Scholarship Credit, it is not limited to two years.

NOTE: You can only claim one of these credits for the same student in the same year. Check www.irs.gov for more information on government loans and credits.

...avoid consequences of a default.

Finally..............................

REMEMBER! You MUST pay back all loans you take. Serious consequences can result if you default on loans including damage to your credit rating, ability to borrow in the future and even legal action.

Notes:

7

Credit, Credit Scores, Credit Cards....

CHARGE!

Most people can't wait to get their first credit card so they can rush off to buy something, anything they want without worrying about having the cash to pay for it. Unfortunately, this soon becomes a habit and we start racking up the charges, don't pay them off on time and get into financial trouble. Aside from building a big bill you can't pay back, you are establishing your CREDIT SCORE. This chapter explains:

- ❒ some of the basics of using a credit card,
- ❒ why you should care about it and,
- ❒ what a credit score is,
- ❒ what to do if you need to fix yours!

Notes:

POP QUIZ!!! (get out those #2 pencils....)

1. You received two offers in the mail for credit cards, one has no annual fee and the other has a fee but you get all sorts of AWESOME rewards. You say:
   a. No fee please.
   b. Bring on those rewards!!!
2. You want to buy a $4.79 latte at a local coffee bar but you're short on cash so you:
   a. Skip it and go to the bagel shop next door and buy one for $1.25 instead.
   b. Charge it on your credit card.
3. Your credit card bill comes and you owe $378. When you sit down to pay your bill you:
   a. Pay the entire bill.
   b. Pay the minimum amount required ($15) and figure you'll pay the rest some other time.
4. You are behind on paying your student loan. You say:
   a. Who cares, I always had to wait forever to get a refund check from my school, now they can wait a little
   b. I'll pay it later; I want to go to Vegas.
   c. Oh Crap! I better stop slacking and make the payments.
5. The cute sorority girl or fraternity boy in your class needs people to sign up for credit cards to raise money. With a smile they ask you to open one. You:
   a. Open 3 thinking you'll have a greater chance for a date.
   b. Open just 1 thinking, "I'll just open it and never use it or cancel it right away."
   c. Politely decline stating that you already have a credit card.
6. You know the following scores: (circle all that apply)
   a. Your favorite team's last game
   b. Your GPA
   c. Your SAT's
   d. Your FICO
7. Your FICO score can effect your:
   a. Ability to get a new car
   b. Ability to get a cell-phone
   c. Ability to get a house
   d. All of the above

ANSWERS:
1. It depends 2. It depends 3. It depends 4. C 5. C 6. all of the above 7. D

Notes:

Explanations:

You are probably thinking, "What's the deal? How can so many questions not have definitive answers?" Well, like your English classes, your FICO score and related matters are subjective. In other words, a lot of it depends on you as an individual, choices you've made, and money you already have or don't have.

The following explanations can help serve as a guide to you when thinking about your own personal financial status. After you read through the explanations, it would be a good idea to look back over your initial answers and decide personally whether they were right or wrong for you!

1 When it comes to credit cards, the general rule is that you should never charge more than what you can afford to pay off in total each month. Unless you are sure that you are going to have endless resources or win the lottery next week. As a college student you do not need to have the "awesome" rewards that credit card companies offer. It is much smarter to choose the card with no annual fee, and build up a good credit score, so that later on in life when you are making the big bucks you can then sign up for a credit card with those fancy rewards. Why pay the extra $70 now – think of all the pizza that could buy.

2 There's really no right or wrong answer to this one except to say that sometimes you have to stop and think whether or not you really "need" it or you just "want" it. Ask yourself if you could manage without it and be better off without the additional expense.

3 Each month that you don't pay your entire bill, the amount you have to pay the following month grows because of the interest charges on the unpaid amount. This happens even if you don't charge anything new. Therefore, keep track of those purchases!! 10 bagels and coffees at $4.79 each is already almost $50!!

4 This is one of the few questions with the obvious answers. Soon I will start to talk all about credit scores and it is important for you to know how much they affect you and what affects them. Even your student debt (one of the better debts to have) is reported to credit bureaus, so make sure to put vacation plans aside and pay those bills.

5 Your credit score is directly related to the number of credit cards and accounts you have, even if you have a zero balance and have never missed a payment. Rule of thumb is to **have as few accounts as possible.**

It is better to stick to one credit card and maybe one retail card when you are in college. This way you can manage all your finances successfully and not have to worry about overlap. What you do on one credit card impacts your entire credit. Also, a lot of new cards can make lenders nervous.

However, it is extremely important that you always pay your bills on time. Therefore, if all you can manage to pay for one month is the minimum payment, then **make sure you pay it on time.**

6 Honestly, most people don't know their FICO (Credit Score). But you should. This three-digit score will soon become more important to you than last night's ball game score.

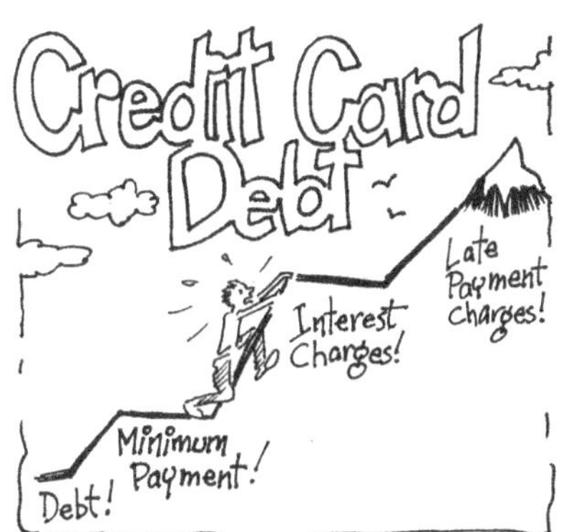

7 Credit scores can affect everything in your life that involves the exchange of money!! That's why you need to know what your FICO score is.!!! Read on!

Notes:

What's The Big Deal About Credit Scores?

Your credit rating affects everything you do financially - from the cost of car insurance to being able to buy a car, get a good rate on a loan for school, car or even buy a house down the road. Some employers even order credit reports to see if you are financially responsible and would be a good hire.

Every time you spend money, pay bills, take out loans or open an account, your credit rating is affected. It is important to make sure your rating is accurate. People with good credit ratings get lower interest rates when they borrow money. That's because they're considered to be better risks by lenders. The lenders believe those people will pay back loans on time.

Companies assign points to these different financial activities and then come up with a composite "Credit Score". This notorious number can mean the difference between being able to buy a car or home and how much you pay for it.
The higher your credit score is, the better it is.

Who would you rather be:

Both individuals below are same age, same job and rent an apartment in same town.

Mr. No Debt
Has two credit cards, no outstanding debt, paid all bills on time and has not missed a loan repayment may get a 5% interest rate on a car loan

Ms. Buy It All
Has five credit cards, owes the most on two and has been late on 1, opened a new loan to help pay off a college loan and missed a payment or two on her old loan. Is turned down by one car lender and gets a whopping 10% interest rate on her car loan.

What Is A Credit Report?

Here's What You Need to Know:

- A credit file disclosure provides you with all the information in your credit file. It includes a list of everyone who has received a credit report about you from the consumer credit reporting agency within a certain time period.
- You're entitled to receive one free credit file disclosure every 12 months from each of the nationwide consumer credit reporting companies. If you want to get your credit report more often you'll have to pay for it
- Residents of some states are eligible for a free credit file disclosure under state law. The following states have laws that make free credit reports available to consumers: Colorado, Georgia, Maine, Maryland, Massachusetts, New Jersey and Vermont.
- If you find a mistake on your credit report, contact the agency and have it corrected! This is important! Even the smallest error could seriously hurt your credit chances. If you find a mistake, send a separate letter to each agency where a mistake is found. Be sure to explain the situation in detail and include a copy of the credit report with the incorrect information highlighted.

What Is A Good Credit Score?

Now that you know what a credit score is and why it's important to protect your credit rating, how do you know whether or not your credit score is good or bad?

...most credit scores range from 300 to 850.

Credit bureaus calculate your score by assigning points to different factors. They then add up the points and come up with a score. Each company has its own formula for the final score but in general, most credit scores range from 300 to 850. Lenders consider lower scores (below 500) riskier so you may not be able to get loans or if you do, you will pay more for them. The higher the score (at least 720) means you are considered a good risk and you will have more options on borrowing and pay less on the money you borrow.

Most people fall somewhere in between but most experts agree that you should try to aim for over 720. It is important to remember that your score is changing all the time and you make the number go up or down depending on how you manage your money. The major influences and their impact on your credit score include:

✔ Payment history – how timely you make your payments

✔ Outstanding debt – how much you owe on each of your loans

Notes:

...it's okay to request your credit score.

✔Length of your credit history – the longer you've had a credit history the better

✔Recent inquiries on your credit report – the number and frequency of inquiries on your account

✔Types of credit in use – how many cards, loans and types of loan

HELP! How Can I Improve My Credit Score?

You can always make changes to improve your credit score. Check off how many you already handle responsibly:

- ❒ Pay your bills on time.
- ❒ If you have missed payments, get current and stay current.
- ❒ Keep balances low on credit cards
- ❒ Pay off debt rather than moving it around.
- ❒ Don't open a number of new credit cards that you don't need.
- ❒ Do your rate shopping for a given loan within a focused period of time.
- ❒ Note that it's OK to request and check your own credit report.
- ❒ It's ok to have credit cards and loans- but manage them responsibly.
- ❒ Note that closing an account doesn't make it go away and will still count as a credit line.

If all else fails and you cannot manage this on your own, contact your creditors or see a legitimate credit counselor. This won't improve your score immediately, but if you can begin to manage your credit and pay on time, your score will get better over time.

Order your credit report today

You can purchase a credit score by contacting one of the nationwide consumer credit reporting companies:

Equifax - www.equifax.com
Experian - www.experian.com
TransUnion - www.transunion.com

Your Own Credit/Debt Worksheet

Take a minute to fill out the credit worksheet to see where you stand. Don't panic if your balance starts adding up, there is always time and people who can help you get back on the right track.

Credit Card or Loan	Date Opened	Amount Owed	Interest Rate

Smart Money Tips

Every teenager and young adult can't wait to get that first credit card. When you get it, use it responsibly. Follow these 3 important tips:

1. Think before you use it. Do you really need to make that purchase? If you can't pay cash, should you really buy it now or wait until you can pay for it in full?

2. If you do use it, PAY IT ON TIME! Paying late results in late charges that add up very quickly. Late payments also affect your credit score!

3. If you can't pay the whole bill, pay as much as you can each month until it is paid off. Try not to make additional charges until all the old ones are paid off.

A Few Tips About Borrowing Money

Before you sign on the dotted line, consider the following:

1. Can you afford to make the monthly payments EVERY month without missing a payment?

2. If you can find a loan with ZERO percent financing, you are probably better off taking that loan, even if the item costs slightly more.

3. Don't co-sign a loan for anyone else, EVER unless you are ready to pay it back for him or her!!!!!

4. Loans add up and have to be paid back. They can destroy your credit rating and make it impossible to start a business, buy a house or car or even purchase low cost insurance.

Notes:

8

Employee Benefits

Notes:

... you may be able to negotiate a higher salary for benefits you don't need.

Compensation is More than Salary

Getting a job means you are going to make money. You are also going to receive additional compensation in the form of benefits. Company benefits cost employers a significant amount of money and may add as much as 35% on to the total cost for a typical employee. That is why some employers may be cutting back on benefits they are offering. They are important to you because they provide financial protection and sometimes additional income at little or no cost to you. In most cases, it is a good financial decision to utilize as many of these benefits as possible.

Basic concepts regarding benefits:

- ❐ Take the time to review your benefit package. If you do not understand something, ask the Human Resources or Benefits Specialist at your company.
- ❐ Part-time employees may not be eligible for benefits.
- ❐ Benefits may not be available unless you work 30 hours a week.
- ❐ The employer pays for some benefits, some you pay for yourself. You should calculate the overall costs before you decide which ones you are signing up for.
- ❐ Pay for most benefits you select from your Before-Tax dollars to reduce your tax liability.
- ❐ Some employees have to wait a period of time before they can enroll. Enroll as soon as you can.
- ❐ Some benefits are portable (you can take them with you if you change jobs). Other benefits end as soon as you leave the employer.
- ❐ Not all employers offer benefits.
- ❐ When looking for a job, you may have to consider whether you need benefits or not. Sometimes a job pays a lower salary if you get benefits. Consider the overall cost benefit to you. If you don't need the benefits, you may be able to negotiate a higher salary.

Benefit Menu

Companies offer a variety of benefits. Some are voluntary (meaning you pay for them yourself if you decide to enroll) and others are mandatory (the employer pays for the benefit and everyone is automatically enrolled). How many of these are offered by your employer and how many are you enrolled in?

- ❐ Health or Medical Insurance
- ❐ Dental Insurance
- ❐ Vision Insurance
- ❐ Short Term Disability Insurance
- ❐ Long Term Disability Insurance
- ❐ Life Insurance

- ❒ Spouse and/or Dependent Life Insurance
- ❒ Long Term Care Insurance
- ❒ Legal Services
- ❒ Flexible Spending Account
- ❒ 401k or 403b Retirement Savings Plan
- ❒ Tuition Reimbursement
- ❒ Stock Savings Plan
- ❒ Car or Home Insurance

We will talk more about those benefits worth considering at this point in your life. The ones we don't discuss you should pursue with your company Benefits Specialist. They may not be worth using your dollars for at this time in your life.

Benefits Definitely Worth Considering

Health Insurance

QUIZ TIME!
Since this will be the most expensive benefit you select, we are going to test your basic knowledge of Health Benefits

Answer True or False for each statement.

1. Health care costs are rising annually.
   True____ False____
2. Employers are paying more for these benefits so you don't have to pay as much.
   True____ False____
3. You don't need to purchase this coverage if you are a student in college. (hint, this is a tricky one)
   True____ False____
4. There are many kinds of health insurance plans and some employers offer more than one to choose from.
   True____ False____

Answers:

1. **True.** Health care costs are rising annually, sometimes as much as 15% to 25% due to increasing medical costs, malpractice insurance and uninsured consumers.
2. **False.** Employers can no longer afford to absorb the costs and are passing the increases on to the workers. Therefore, your costs go up, or your benefits go down.
3. **False.** Depending on your age, your parent's policy and family decisions, you may or may not need this coverage. You must discuss this with your family and determine if you are covered. **You must have health insurance.** One other word on availability. If you don't work and you are not covered by your

Notes:

parent's policy, you may be able to purchase a basic policy through your college. Check with your college.

4. **True.** This is a fairly confusing benefit. Work with the benefit specialist at your job. To give you a basic understanding, look at the following types of health insurance plans that companies are offering today:

   - ✔ PPO is usually the most expensive, you go to whichever caregiver you want. This is sometimes called a Traditional Indemnity plan.
   - ✔ HMO generally has a low co-pay, set amount you pay for each visit but you have to use the providers in the group. If you go outside of the providers covered, you pay the entire cost of the bill.
   - ✔ Gatekeeper/No Gatekeeper means you may need a referral.

As a general rule, unless you have a major health problem and your HMO does not cover your specialists, you should enroll in the less expensive plan. The major aspects of the plan to look for are:

- ❐ Does it have a prescription (drug) plan? Unless you take regular medication, this is not a major concern.
- ❐ What is the annual deductible?
- ❐ What is the maximum out of pocket cost? How much will you be required to pay yourself before you have reached the most you will have to pay? This can vary greatly within plans.
- ❐ What is the basic co-pay for Doctor visits? This is the amount you would pay for each visit. Generally, this is an affordable amount and is the cost you will incur most often.
- ❐ What is the most you will have to pay for a hospital stay including all surgical costs? Believe it or not, this is the most important feature of your plan. Health insurance is really intended to provide coverage for catastrophic events such as a major illness, surgery or hospital stay. These costs can run as high as $100,000 for a short hospital stay.
- ❐ As a general rule, determine what plan fits your lifestyle. If you have a family with young children, an HMO might be more cost effective. If you have serious health issues and/or as you age, you may, if you have the option, want to select a plan with additional flexibility for specialists.

For Dental and Vision, you may have to do the math to see if it's worth it. Do you wear glasses and/or go to the eye doctor every year? How much does it cost you?

Vision Care

- ✔ **Cost of glasses and eye exam** __________
- ✔ **Cost of insurance** __________
- ✔ **Which is greater?** __________

If you spend more on insurance, then why would you purchase it?

Dental Care

This one is a little harder to figure out. One broken tooth or filling can make up for the entire annual cost. In most cases, it is worth purchasing the Dental insurance. You should make sure you utilize the benefit by going to the dentist at least annually for a checkup and cleaning. If you find after the first year or two you didn't cover your costs, then drop the coverage.

Disability Income Protection

What is your single most important asset? Your income and your ability to earn an income. Without your income you cannot pay your bills, pay off college loans, take a vacation, save for the future, and simply, you cannot do anything. So the single most important insurance protection to have is disability income protection.

Disability means being unable to work because you have an illness or had an accident/injury. This does not mean work related issues. Are people really missing work because of disability?

YOU BET! Here are some statistics to make you stop and think!

- ✔ **A fatal injury occurs every 5 minutes. A disabling injury occurs every 1.5 seconds.**
  Source: Injury Facts®, 2003

- ✔ **There is a death caused by a motor vehicle crash every 12 minutes. There is a disabling injury every 14 seconds.**
  Source: Injury Facts®, 2003

- ✔ **Income lost through disability is 2 times as great as auto accident losses, and 3 times as great as fire losses.**
  Source: National Safety Council, 2003

- ✔ **Almost 3 in 10 of today's 20-year-olds will become disabled before reaching age 67.**
  Source: Social Security Basic Facts, July 2004

Notes:

✔ **1 in 5 people will be disabled for one year or more before age 65.**

Source: Compton Insurance Marketing, 2002

✔ **For 30-year-old males, the risk of a long-term disability is 4.1 times more likely than the risk of death.**

Source: National Safety Council, 2003

✔ **Nearly half of small employers (5 to 100 workers) believe that the likelihood of an employee becoming disabled is one in 50. The actual likelihood, ACLI reports, is one in three.**

Source: American Council of Life Insurers (ACLI), 2003

Disability insurance pays you an income if you become disabled. There are two types. Short-term and Long-term.

Short Term Disability covers you from the first day you become disabled and lasts for approximately 6 months. It assumes you will be going back to work and will fully recover. Many employers provide this at no cost to you. Depending on the type of plan your company has, it can pay you anywhere from 66 and 2/3 of your salary to your full salary. **Find out what your company offers.**

Long Term Disability is a little different. Like health insurance, it is intended to provide catastrophic coverage in case you suffer from a major illness or accident. This insurance pays you an income for as long as you are disabled and cannot work up to approximately age 65. It only pays a part of your income (approximately 60% of your base salary) and you have to wait 90 to 180 days to start collecting. If your company does not offer this to you, you should purchase it on your own.

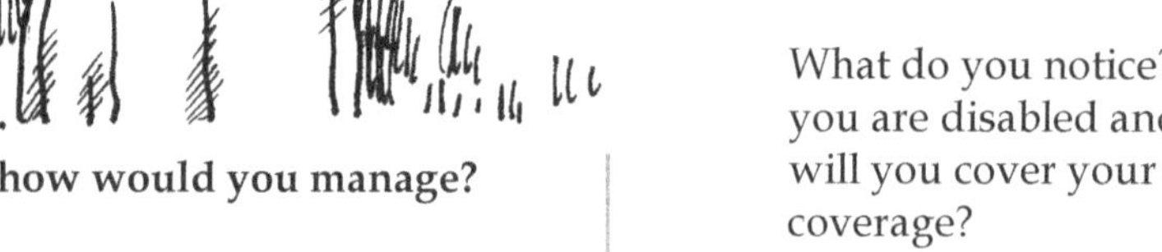

... **how would you manage?**

How would you manage if you were disabled?

✔	Current Salary	$ ________
✔	Current Expenses	$ ________
✔	Salary if you become disabled and cannot work	$ ________
✔	Expenses if you become disabled and cannot work (increase current by 10%)	$ ________

What do you notice? That your expenses are higher when you are disabled and that your income is lower? How will you cover your expenses if you don't have disability coverage?

Life Insurance

Employers sometimes provide a basic life insurance policy for employees at no cost to the employee. It could be a base amount such as $50,000 or an amount equivalent to your salary. Purchasing additional life insurance is a topic of discussion you should have with your insurance professional or a financial advisor you trust. In most cases, additional life insurance would make sense if you had a need to provide financial support for someone else in the event you would die prematurely, or to help pay for funeral burial expenses or outstanding debt you have accumulated.

401k or 403b Retirement Plans

We're going to go into much more detail about these plans in Chapter 11. So for now, just remember this .... DO IT! As soon as you are eligible, start participating. Even if you only do the minimum amount allowed, you must start as soon as possible. Why? For the following reasons:

- ✔ You are using before-tax dollars and are reducing your taxable income.
- ✔ You may receive an employer match on the amount you contribute so it's like getting "free money."
- ✔ Your money grows tax-deferred.
- ✔ Compounding of your earnings and savings will be significant in allowing you to accumulate large sums for retirement.

That's it for now. Chapter 11 goes into much more detail on this VERY important benefit.

Car and Home Insurance

If your company offers reduced costs for these insurance products, get a quote. It may or may not be better than the price you are paying today. Just make sure you are comparing apples to apples. For example, if they quote you with $500 deductible but you currently have a $250 then it isn't a fair comparison.

Flexible Spending Accounts (FSA, Section 125 Plans)

This is a wonderful way to pay for some of your health care costs and other benefits. Remember in Chapter 4 when we talked about keeping more of your salary and paying less tax? Well this is one way you do it. The FSA allows you to have a certain amount of your income put into a special account held by an outside administrator. The money you put in comes off your salary before taxes so you are using before-tax dollars. Every time you have a health care cost that is not covered by your health insurance, you put in a request to have these costs reimbursed to you through your FSA up to the maximum amount you put in.

Notes:

Example: *You have $100 a month put into the FSA account. That totals $1200 a year. Your taxable income is reduced by $1200 and then you get that money back if your health insurance doesn't cover an expense. Basic health care products like analgesics, muscle rub, deodorant, mouthwash, toothpaste, birth control, are all things you can use your FSA for.*

Careful! Try and figure out in advance how much you might have to pay for on your own and then put this amount into the FSA. It's better to **underestimate** the amount to put away so you don't lose it if you don't use it up.

List how many products you generally purchase at your local drugstore, how many doctor visits you have in a year and how much you spend on medications in a year:

Type of Expense	Cost	Amount Covered by Insurance	Net Cost
☐ Doctor Visits ☐ Dentist ☐ Optometrist ☐ Specialist			
☐ Medications ☐ ________			
☐ Monthly Drugstore Purchases ☐ ________			
		Total Annual Out-of-Pocket Cost	$______

...on some financial decisions.

The Total Annual Out of Pocket Costs should be the approximate amount you might want to contribute to your FSA plan. If you aren't sure, round down and put in a little less. Congratulations! This is a sound, sensible financial decision!

Smart Money Tips

- ✔ Some of your benefits will be offered through Payroll Deduction. This means they will take the cost of the benefit out of your payroll and it is intended to be a payment convenience for you.
- ✔ Review your benefit package each year because the benefits change. Make sure you learn about the changes and select what is appropriate for you at that time. Life is dynamic and your situation will always change. Make sure your benefits keep current with your personal needs.
- ✔ Do the cost analysis to make sure the benefit works for you
- ✔ Consider benefits an extension of your compensation package. It could be worth an additional $5,000 or more a year.
- ✔ Nobody wants to purchase insurance. You can only purchase insurance when you don't need it. When you're healthy you can qualify for it. When you aren't, you can't get it. The younger you are when you purchase it, the less it costs. So, from a smart money perspective, buy the kinds of insurance you need when you are young and healthy.
- ✔ If your company offers a 401K or 403b plan, find out what the most they will match is and then contribute at least that amount. If you can afford more, consider increasing the amount you contribute periodically until you reach the maximum.
- ✔ Don't forget to also save additional money outside of your company 401k plan since that one is intended for retirement. You will also need to save money that is available to you for emergency situations or for big purchases.

Notes:

9
Insurance Basics

Notes:

...insurance is a top priority.

Why Insurance Now?

Insurance is one of those things that nobody wants to have to think about, understand and least of all, pay for. Unfortunately, without it, you put yourself at serious financial risk. Take the following quiz and see why you should make obtaining the proper insurance one or your top financial objectives.

1. I will be covered by my parent's health insurance plan until I get a job and have my own.
   True or False
2. Car insurance costs more for the following:
   a. People who drive sports cars
   b. People with tickets or accidents
   c. People who live in cities
   d. People who drive to work instead of taking public transportation
   e. All of the above
3. Renter insurance pays if someone has a claim due to:
   a. A fire in their apartment and their property is ruined
   b. Someone falls and gets hurt in your apartment
   c. Your TV, Computer and DVD player are stolen
   d. Your sink overflows and ruins the floor in your apartment
   e. A,B,C
   f. All of the above
4. Life insurance can always be purchased. **True or False**
5. If you become disabled and cannot work:
   a. Your income goes up because you get disability payments from your job
   b. Your expenses go down because you no longer spend as much
   c. You can get a loan to cover your expenses
   d. You don't have to worry because someone will take care of everything for you
   e. None of the above

Answers:

1. Health Insurance

I will be covered by my parent's health insurance plan until I get a job and have my own.
Answer – False!

Individuals are generally covered from birth to age 19 as a dependent child. Once you turn 19, you must be a full-time student and unmarried to continue to be covered as a dependent child. This continues as long as you are a full-time student to age 23.

Not all insurance companies use these guidelines however 19/23 is the norm and you should check with your parent's employer plan.

There are also state mandates and specific employer provisions that may broaden coverage and make it more available to older dependents. Once again, you must check with your parent's employer plan. **You don't want to be caught without health insurance!**

If you do not have coverage through your parent's policy, you **must** make sure you have health insurance coverage. We all hope to stay healthy and not need care but even the simplest emergency visit to a hospital can end up costing thousands of dollars. This could have a devastating financial impact on your financial future.

Here's what you need to know about health insurance:

- ❒ Find out if you are covered by your parent's plan
- ❒ If you work, find out if you work enough hours to be eligible for your company plan if they offer one.
- ❒ If you are eligible find out what your employer offers and how much it costs
- ❒ Make sure you have coverage

...make sure you have health insurance.

There are two major types of plans:

1. Health Maintenance Organizations
2. Preferred Provider Organizations

Health Maintenance Organizations (HMO)s

You pay a monthly fee and are required to use the physicians, hospitals, and health care providers that belong to this organization.

This is usually the less expensive choice but has more limitations. It's a good choice if you don't care about having choice in selection of providers and you want lower costs.

Preferred Provider Organizations (PPOs)

This type of plan gives you more choice in selection of your health care provider. The plan generally pays different costs depending on whether the provider you select participates in your plan or not. This plan generally costs more than the HMO.

Basic Coverage Provided

Both HMO and PPO plans normally provide access to the following services:

1. **Hospitalization (facility)** - covers expenses for hospitalization, lab tests, surgical procedures and visits to doctors.

2. **Providers** - covers most medical costs up to a lifetime maximum (this varies by plan) for doctor visits and other health care providers.

3. **Prescription Plans** – Covers costs for medications that you take. There are usually at least two levels, generic and name brand. You pay more for name brand medications however not all medications have generic versions. You can check with your pharmacist and ask your doctor when the prescription is prescribed to see if you can substitute it with a generic to save money.

...what costs are covered?

Notes:

Key Terms To Know

- ❐ **Deductibles:** this is the amount you pay out of your own pocket before the insurance company starts to pay for the claim. This amount varies by plan and the lower the deductible, the higher the premium. You have to decide whether you prefer to pay more out of pocket in the event you have a claim or more out of your paycheck to pay for the insurance.
- ❐ **Co-Insurance:** this is the amount that you pay over the deductible. It is usually a percentage such as 20% or 30%. **Example:** You pay 20% of all expenses over $100 deductible and the insurance company pays 80%. So if the bill is $10,000, you pay $100 deductible plus 20% of $9,900 or $ 2,080. The insurance company pays the rest.
- ❐ **Co-Payments:** A fixed dollar amount required when seeing a doctor. For example, a $20 co-pay each time you visit the doctor.

You really have to make the effort to understand the plans you are offered. TAKE THE TIME to determine which plan works best for you. The difference in plans is usually:

- ❐ How much you will have to pay out of pocket yourself
- ❐ What "extras" or supplemental coverage a plan offers
- ❐ Which provider's participate in your plan
- ❐ How easy or difficult it is to collect on a claim
- ❐ How good the service is

Do You Have Health Insurance?

Take a moment to fill out this chart with the most important features of your plan. There are more features but these are the most important.

Feature	What Your Plan Provides
Insurance Company	
Basic Type HMO or POS or PPO	
Gatekeeper (Yes or No)	
Prescription plan (Yes or No)	
Prescription Co-pay	
Doctor Visit Co-pay	
Co-Insurance (example 70%, 80%)	
Maximum Out of Pocket (example $1,000)	
Emergency Room Co-pay	

Let's review some very basic principles of health insurance:

- ❒ Most employers offer some type of health insurance. This is usually the best way to obtain health insurance. Employers may pay for some portion of the expense but don't count on it. Costs are going up each year and some employers are rapidly decreasing the amount they will pay.
- ❒ Dental bills are usually not covered by health insurance policies but some may include some types of dental surgeries. You may want to consider purchasing dental insurance if your circumstance and income warrants it.
- ❒ Make sure you understand the deductibles and co-pay provisions. This will determine much of the expense you have to pay out-of-pocket.
- ❒ Find out if you need referrals to see another doctor before you schedule an appointment. Some plans have gatekeeper provisions that require you to get approval in order to be paid for the visit.

Smart Money Tip

Health insurance will be the largest insurance expense you have so it pays to take the time to research it, understand it and make the smartest financial decision.

2. Car Insurance

Car insurance costs more for the following: a. People who drive sports cars; b. People with tickets or accidents; c. People who live in cities; d. People who drive to work instead of taking public transportation; or, e. All of the above.

Answer E - All of the Above.

Car insurance can be very expensive and the cost is dependent on a number of factors. Primarily, **all the answers in question 2 affect the price you pay for insurance.**

Do any of these apply to you?

- ❒ The younger you are, the more you will pay. This usually changes when you turn 30 or get married. Younger males pay more than younger females, sorry guys.
- ❒ People who drive high performance or higher value vehicles pay more,
- ❒ People who drive longer distances pay more than those who barely use the car
- ❒ People who live in higher density populated areas such as cities pay more than those who live in rural areas.
- ❒ Finally, and probably most obviously, people who have had accidents and/ or tickets pay the most.

Don't feel singled out. All these costs are based on actuarial statistics. Insurance companies spend lots of money trying to figure out how to create their rates so they don't lose money. They also have to make sure the rates they charge are fair and non-discriminatory. Insurance is a highly regulated industry.

...car insurance can be expensive.

Notes:

From the day you receive your learner's permit and either own a car or live in a house that has a car, you will have car insurance. People have car insurance because of two reasons:

1. IT'S THE LAW!
2. You want to protect yourself financially in the event of an accident.

Basic Car Insurance Coverage

Liability Coverage

Protects you from lawsuits if someone is injured or their car is damaged in an accident that is your fault. Each state has minimum amounts you are required to purchase. If you can afford it, buy higher amounts because people sue for very high damages that the minimums usually don't cover. This coverage is usually mandatory, required by the state.

- ✔ **Bodily Injury Liability** – pays for expenses you cause and if you injure someone
- ✔ **Property Damage Liability** – pays if you damage someone else's property

Physical Damage Coverage

Covers the damage to your vehicle for either theft, glass breakage or other "physical damages" to your vehicle. This coverage usually has a deductible or amount you have to pay out of pocket before the insurance company will pay. This amount varies but the higher the deductible, the lower your costs. This coverage is optional unless you have a loan on your car.

- ✔ **Collision Coverage** – pays for damages to your car due to accident
- ✔ **Comprehensive Coverage** – pays for damages to your car due to non-accident related, usually like windshield damages or theft

Uninsured Motorist Coverage

This is mandatory coverage that protects you and pays your medical costs in case you are injured in an accident by someone who does not have car insurance. It is usually the same limit amounts as your liability coverage.

No-Fault Laws

Under no-fault laws, your own company pays for the damages and it doesn't matter who caused the accident. The cost for this is built into the policy. However, don't be fooled by the term No

Fault. You will still get charged extra if it is your fault. The only difference is how the insurance company settles the claim.

What do you know about your car insurance policy?

Filling this out can help you save money$!$!$!$!

Feature	Your Car Insurance Policy
Name of Insurance Company	
Name of Insurance Agent	
Liability Limits	
Collision Deductible	
Comprehensive Deductible	
Uninsured Motorist Coverage	
No Fault? Yes or No	
Points on your Policy?	
Any discounts?	

Smart Money Tips

- ❐ Comparison shop your car insurance
- ❐ Avoid high performance, high cost cars if you want to save money on your insurance rates
- ❐ Drive safely and avoid tickets/accidents
- ❐ Consider location of employment when you take a job, working closer to home may keep insurance costs down.
- ❐ Make sure you have adequate coverage but keep deductibles as high as you can afford to contain costs

When was the last time you shopped your car insurance and got a quote? You should get a quote at least every other year. Make sure you check at least three companies.

3. Renter Insurance

Renter insurance pays if someone has a claim due to: a. A fire in their apartment and their property is ruined; b. Someone falls and gets hurt in your apartment; c. Your TV, Computer and DVD player are stolen; d. Your sink overflows and ruins the floor in your apartment; e. A,B,C; or, f. All of the above.
Answer E – A, B and C.

Renter insurance protects losses to your personal property where you live. So if you rent, you should consider purchasing renter insurance to protect all the things you own that you worked hard to purchase.

Why do You Need Renter Insurance?

How many hours did you have to work to pay for that big screen TV you purchased or the Prada pocketbook you bought? Too many? Well if there is a fire in your home that destroys these items or someone manages to break in and take some of your prized possessions, renter insurance would pay for your losses … sounds good doesn't it?

... protect your belongings!

But that's not all..................

Sue, Sue, Sue .... no, that's not the nickname for three girls named Susan. That's what people may do if they get hurt on your property. They sue you so they can get money from you because they were injured and you are held responsible or liable. Here's where renter insurance comes to the rescue once again. The liability portion from the insurance coverage will pay for damages if someone is hurt on your property and you are found liable. These costs can be thousands and even millions of dollars.

Think it's too expensive to own? NOPE! Depending on how much coverage you purchase and where you live, renter insurance can be as low as $10 a month. It really is VERY affordable and you shouldn't be without it!

Make a list of all your valuables and put it in a safe place. List how much each item cost. Take pictures of the highest price items. This will help prove you owned it if it is lost.

ITEM	COST
Furniture	
Kitchen	
Electronics	
Clothing	

Smart Money Tips

- ❒ Renter Insurance is INEXPENSIVE and valuable!
- ❒ Losing property due to theft, fire or some other damages can cost thousands to replace.
- ❒ People do sometimes have reason to sue. Protect yourself with insurance

- ❐ Renter insurance does not cover damages to the structure itself, just your possessions. So if the walls or floors are damaged, it won't be covered. The landlord or owner should have insurance for that.

4. Life Insurance

Life insurance can always be purchased.
Answer – False!

No way! People can only buy life insurance when they are healthy. If you have a serious health problem, you will either have to pay a lot to buy the insurance or you cannot buy it at all.

So what is life insurance anyway?

Life insurance is a type of insurance coverage where you purchase an amount of coverage, let's say $100,000 and when you die (notice there are no if's here), the person you designated as your beneficiary, will receive that amount.

...buy life insurance when you are healthy.

Why People Buy Life Insurance

People generally consider buying life insurance once they are married or have someone who is dependent on them. However, there are other times when you might consider purchasing it so let's review why:

1. To provide money for someone else who is dependent on you.
2. It may be required by a bank or for a loan you take on your car or home.
3. To make sure you have some for the future so if your health changes, you will always have some coverage.
4. Your employer may offer it and you will want to take advantage of the benefit.
   (See chapter 8 on Employee Benefits)

Type of Life Insurance

There are two basic types of life insurance, Term and Permanent. The differences can be viewed much like buying or leasing a car or renting or owning a house.

Term Insurance

Like cars and homes, when you rent or lease, you don't have any equity. You pay a monthly amount and when you stop, you are finished with the car or apartment. That's term insurance. You pay a premium for a period of time or term and when you stop, the insurance policy is finished and you no longer have it or the coverage it provided. The advantage is it is usually much less expensive.

Notes:

Permanent Insurance

Unlike term insurance, the permanent insurance lasts forever. Eventually, someone will receive the money from it. It also builds equity, what you build when you own a house, called "Cash Value." The cash value grows annually through interest or dividend payments depending on the type of permanent insurance you purchase. You may be able to access the cash value through policy loans and withdrawals. These withdrawals and loans will reduce the policy death benefit and may impact the premiums you pay. It is important to discuss the use of your life insurance cash values with an insurance professional before making any changes.

Smart Money Tips

- ❐ Determine what your employer gives you for free first
- ❐ Consider purchasing a basic term insurance policy when you are young to lock in rates when the price is very low. Once you purchase, the price is usually locked in.
- ❐ Review your needs every year or two to see if you should purchase more insurance
- ❐ Usually a combination of term and permanent insurance is best

Don't ever let anyone tell you, you don't or won't need life insurance. Your reasons for owning it will change over the years but no one ever regretted having purchased it. The biggest regrets are always held by those left behind without enough money to live on or for not buying it when you are younger and healthy because it so inexpensive then. Usually you can convert term insurance policies to permanent insurance policies, so start with the inexpensive term insurance if that's all you can afford.

5. Disability Insurance

If you become disabled and cannot work: a. Your income goes up because you get disability payments from your job; b. Your expenses go down because you no longer spend as much; c. You can get a loan to cover your expenses; d. You don't have to worry because someone will take care of everything for you; or, e. None of the above.

Answer E – None of the Above!

As we already discussed in Chapter 8 – Benefits, your income is your most important asset. When you are disabled, your expenses go up, your income goes down and everything in your life changes!

What exactly do we mean by disabled? Think about whether or not you know someone who had one of these experiences:

- ❐ Bad skiing accident and broke a leg or arm
- ❐ Car accident and was in the hospital and couldn't work

- ❒ Developed a serious health problem such as cancer or heart disease
- ❒ Had a baby and had complications during the pregnancy and had to stay in bed
- ❒ Developed HIV or AIDs and couldn't work
- ❒ Had a severe case of mononucleosis and had to stay in bed for months

These are just a few of the hundreds if not thousands of situations that could cause a person to have to miss work for weeks or months and yes, for years. Some people are so disabled that they can never work another day of their life!

...what if you are disabled?

Let's do an exercise. Fill out the following worksheet and see what happens to your expenses when you are disabled:

Type Of Expense	Expenses While Working	Expenses While Disabled
Rent/Mortgage		
Utilities		
Car loan/lease		
Student loans		
Credit Card bills		
Food		
Prescriptions		
Doctor Bills		
Telephone Bills		
Insurance Payments		
Gas for Car		
Personal Care		
TOTAL		

Most likely, your expenses while disabled are higher than expenses while working!

Now, do the next exercise to figure out your income while you **cannot** work due to injury or illness.

Income Sources	While Working	While Disabled
Salary		
State Disability Insurance		
Group Insurance from Work		
Personal Insurance		
TOTAL INCOME		

Notice how your income is lower while disabled than while working? So now take the final step. Subtract your expenses while disabled from your income while disabled. **If the answer is a negative number, you have a problem.**

Notes:

The answer is probably a negative number or a deficit. This means you won't have enough money to cover your expenses if you become disabled.

Where will you get the money?

- ❐ Use your savings?
- ❐ Go back to living with your family?
- ❐ Borrow money from friends or family?
- ❐ Get a loan?
- ❐ Go back to work even if you are not ready physically or mentally?

Most of these solutions don't work! Many people don't have enough money saved to cover even one month of expenses. Do you really want to live with your family again? Who do you know who could afford to loan you money and would actually be willing to? Banks are reluctant to give loans to people who may not be able to pay them back. Going back to work when you aren't ready is not a good idea as you may endanger yourself or someone else.

So What Should You Do?!?!?!?!

Make sure you have adequate disability income protection. Many jobs offer this benefit and if they make extra coverage available, buy it! If your employer does not offer it, try to purchase some yourself.

Smart Money Tips

- ❐ Disability Income Protection is the most important insurance you should have next to health insurance.
- ❐ You can only buy insurance when you are healthy, before you become disabled so **make sure you have some.**
- ❐ You can only buy it when you work full-time (more than 30 hours)
- ❐ The price is higher for smokers … don't smoke!
- ❐ Disability insurance costs much less than health insurance and is a necessary expense.

Without your income, you can't do anything so protect it!

Financially responsible people purchase insurance. It protects your assets, your family, your income and your future. Talk to an insurance professional to get more information on the different types of insurance you are interested in and should have available to you if you need it.

10

Investment 101

Notes:

Money to Invest

We assume that by reading this book you have a desire to manage your finances and to enjoy financial success now and into the future. We've already discussed the importance of understanding the difference between **needs** and **wants**. Hopefully, you have accepted the belief that making sensible financial decisions will help you to achieve the financial and personal goals you desire. Let's take a moment to think about and make a short list of the financial goals you might have at this stage in your life:

Financial Goals

GOAL	How Much Money You Will Need	Time Frame
Example: Pay off College Loans	$25,000	10 Years
Example: Save for a house	$35,000	5 Years
Add Others Below:		
Annual Income		
Savings		
Retirement		

...learn investments concepts.

Once you have financial goals, it's important to utilize basic financial principles to manage your money effectively. You will need to figure out how to achieve the financial goals you have listed above. These goals will change over time as well as the amount of money you will need to accomplish each of them. Revisit these goals periodically.

You should know some of the concepts associated with investing and saving to help you decide how to position the money you have managed to accumulate and plan to accumulate over your lifetime.

Smart people use more than one investment method for their money. They usually have different buckets of money put aside for different purposes.

Let's look at each bucket.

Emergency

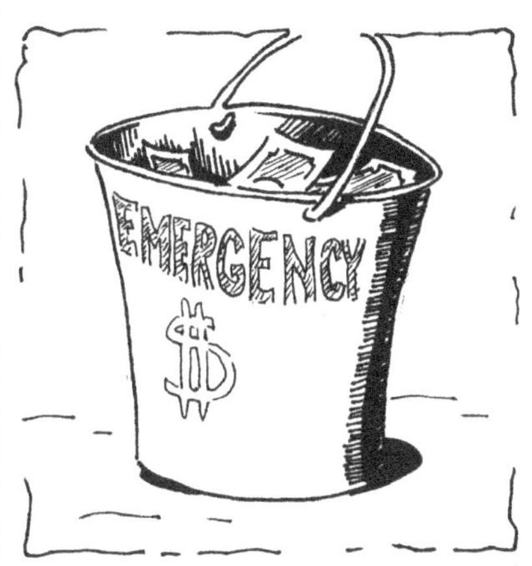

This bucket has money that you need to keep liquid (can access and use immediately). Most people like to keep emergency money very safe, meaning not subject to unnecessary risk so they don't lose any of it. This money is set aside for emergencies, such as:

- ✔ getting a bill for a repair you didn't expect, getting in a car accident and needing money right away,
- ✔ having to go somewhere for a family or medical emergency.

This money doesn't usually grow quickly from investment returns. It is just there so you have it when you need it. A common rule of thumb has been three to six months worth of living expenses. However the exact amount you decide to keep in this bucket is largely a personal decision.

List three things you might need emergency money for and how much you will need for each.

	Emergency Need	How Much Money
1.	______________________	______________________
2.	______________________	______________________
3.	______________________	______________________

Accumulation

This bucket is used to hold money that you don't need immediately but will need within 5 to 10 years to possibly make a large purchase such as a car, house or even pay for college. It's money that you want to grow at a moderate rate but are not willing to subject to too much risk because you don't want to lose it. Because you have 5 to 10 years until you need it, you can take a little more risk because if the value goes down, you may have time for it to go back up before you need to use it.

List 3 things you might want to accumulate large sums of money for, how much and how many years until you need it.

	Purchase	Cost	When Needed
1.	______________	______________	______________
2.	______________	______________	______________
3.	______________	______________	______________

Retirement

This is the bucket you probably don't want to think about too much at this time in your life but the reality is, it is the bucket that you will need the most and for the longest period of time in your life. It's also the bucket that if you start putting money in now, will grow the most substantially. It generally may be well over 30, 40 or even 50 years before you need this money so you may be willing to take the most risk with it and invest it most aggressively (especially if you are younger and have more time to overcome a potential loss). Chapter 11 will talk more about Retirement Savings.

At what age do you plan to retire?________________________
How much money do you think you'll need to cover your expenses each year in today's dollars? ____________________

____

Speculative

Okay, this is the "fun" bucket. The one where everyone wants to "INVEST". Get rich quick! Buy stocks, invest in friend's businesses, etc. This is the bucket of money that you have to be prepared to lose. Speculative money is money that if you lose, you can say, "oh well", I really didn't need it and it was fun taking the chance! Why is that? It's because speculative investments are things that have the most risk, are most likely to lose money. It is true that when they are successful, you can make a lot of money as well. Just be sure that you have already set aside enough for the first three buckets before you put any money into the speculative buckets.

How much money are you willing to lose if your investment is a "failure?"

If you're not prepared to say all of it, then you might need to reconsider how much of your "hard-earned" money you invest this way.

Notes:

So Where Should I Put My Money?

People always want advice on what they should do with their money? How should they invest it? To answer these questions, you first have to do some homework, learn some basic concepts and answer the following questions:

1. How long do you have before you need to use the money?
2. How much risk are you willing to take?

Basic Concepts

- ✔ **Time Horizon**
- ✔ **Risk Tolerance**
- ✔ **Asset Allocation**
- ✔ **Rate of Return**

...what if your investment is a loser?

Time Horizon

This is how long it will be until you need to use the money. The longer the time horizon, the more risk you can historically take. The shorter the time horizon, the less risk you might want to take.

The first rule in investing is to know your time frame. Is your time frame immediate, short term or long term? In other words, how long will it be until you need to use the money? This is important because you make different investment decisions based on how much time you have to accumulate the money.

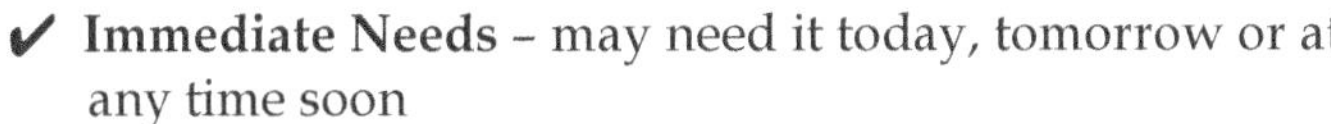

- ✔ **Immediate Needs** – may need it today, tomorrow or at any time soon
- ✔ **Short Term Goals** – 5 to 10 years
- ✔ **Long Term Goals** – 10 years plus

Risk Tolerance

Every person feels differently about taking chances with their money. Some people love to gamble and some people never do. Some people feel it's worth taking a chance to make more money; other's would rather keep their money buried in their backyard or under their mattress and take no chances at all. Realistically, the majority of people tend to fall somewhere in the middle.
Risk tolerance is a term that is used to evaluate how much risk you are willing to take with your investments in order to get the investment results you want.

The higher the risk, the higher the potential for loss but the higher the possible reward.

Higher the Risk   Higher Potential Loss   Higher Possible Reward

Notes:

The lower the risk, the lower the chance for loss but the lower the possible reward.

Before you make any investment decisions, you should complete a risk tolerance questionnaire to help you figure out how much risk you are willing and prepared to take with the money you are investing. A sample risk tolerance questionnaire is located in the appendix.

Asset Allocation

This is probably the most important concept to understand and generally has the greatest impact on the performance of your investments.

Put simply, asset allocation is the way you divide up your investments, or diversify them among the different asset classes or investment choices. Sounds confusing? Not really. You've heard of the expression "don't put all your eggs in one basket." That's what asset allocation means.

To keep it simple, for right now, you just need to know there are three basic asset classes; Cash, Bonds, and Stocks. The most important thing to know is that most people should use a combination of these three. You SHOULD NOT put all of your money in just one asset class. So if you keep all of your money in a savings account (cash) or all of it is invested in stocks or all of it is in a bond, then you need to talk to a financial professional to see how you should change your strategy. You want to consider diversification!

The reason you need to have a "mix" or diversify is that each of these asset classes reacts to economic conditions differently. Sometimes stocks will make money and bonds will lose. Sometimes it's the reverse. So if you always have a mix of some of each, then you will probably have better performance overall.

Take some time and watch a money management morning news show this weekend. Closely listen to how all the pundits and so-called "experts" cannot agree on any one-asset class. One thing they will almost always agree on is to diversify.

Asset allocation does not guarantee a profit or protect against loss in declining markets. There is no guarantee that a diversified portfolio will outperform a non-diversified portfolio or that diversification among asset classes will reduce risk.

Rate of Return

The term "rate of return," also known as ROR, is one of the most common expressions you'll hear when talking about investments. It is the amount of money or rate that you earn (or lose) on the money you invest. It is expressed as a percentage.

Example:

0% rate of return, 5% rate of return, 10% rate of return 20% rate of return

Don't be fooled … you can also have negative rates of return such as:

-7% rate of return, -15% rate of return and yes, even -22% rate of return

When you see a negative rate of return, the value of your investment has gone down. If you started with $100 and you have a –10% rate of return, you now have only $90. On the other hand, if you have a 10% rate of return, if you started with $100, you now have $110.

ROR is an essential concept and its very important when studying your investments or researching future investment opportunities. The only advice we can give is to do your homework; listen to many differing opinions and to always remember that under life circumstances even the most well thought out strategy can end up in an investment loss. There is always risk and the risk belongs to you alone.

Asset Classes

Here's a very basic overview of the three asset classes and when to use them:

Cash - this is for your "safe" money. This is where people put money they want to be able to access immediately. It is usually low risk but also has a very low rate of return. This is for your immediate money needs. Types of cash accounts include:

- ❒ Savings and Passbook accounts
- ❒ Checking accounts
- ❒ Money Market accounts
- ❒ Certificates of Deposit (CD's)

Bonds - can be used for multiple purposes. Generally, they are considered fairly safe and less risky than stocks. They usually offer a higher rate of return than cash accounts but the value of the bond can go up or down and the rate of return can vary as well. Some people use bonds for retirement income or savings.

Notes:

Stocks – this asset class has more risk and the value of these investments can go up or down. They also have greater chance for higher rates of return and can make you more money than cash accounts and historically bonds. These investments should only be used when your time horizon or need for the money you use is not immediate, or is longer term and you are willing to lose the money you started with. Stocks might be considered investments that are more speculative or higher risk.

Mutual Funds - are a group of stocks or bonds or a mixture of both, grouped together to form one Mutual Fund. Usually, this is a less risky than buying individual stocks or bonds and it also has a chance for higher rates of return than cash. Mutual Funds are generally used for accumulation and retirement goals.

Smart Money Tips

To sum it all up, remember:

- ❐ Figure out what your financial goals are.
- ❐ Organize your financial needs and create a strategy.
- ❐ Complete the Risk Tolerance questionnaire to see how much risk you are willing to take (are you willing to lose money).
- ❐ Determine how soon you need the money.
- ❐ Use asset allocation and diversify where you keep your money.
- ❐ Review your needs periodically.
- ❐ Regularly check the performance of your investments.
- ❐ Read your investment statements and make sure you know how they are doing and learn what they mean .
- ❐ Learn as much as you can.
- ❐ Talk to an investment professional.

11

Retirement

Notes:

But I'm Only a Kid ...

True or False

1. The average American has enough money saved for retirement and will never run out of money.

2. Social Security is intended to provide all your retirement income when you retire.

Answers – False to both.

One day you will want to retire and you may need to have enough money to live on for at least 30 to 40 years of retirement. Think about it. If you retire at age 60 and live to age 100 (don't laugh, more people are living that long and longer), that's 40 years of retirement. In the future, some people may be retired longer than they actually ever worked.

That's a long time that you will need to have enough money to live on. Where do you think this income will come from? What are the sources of income that you can think of for retirement?

Sources of Income

____

____

____

____

Experts often suggest that most people will need at least 80% of their current income to cover their expenses at retirement. Retirement income is usually comprised of three components, pension plans, savings or investment income, and social security.

Why Plan Now?

How much money are you actually saving a week, month or year right now? If you're like many Americans, you are probably not saving anything at all. Sad but true, many Americans spend everything they earn and more, piling up debt, giving little or no thought to retirement.

What this means is that they will not have enough saved for retirement. The majority of your retirement income will come from your personal investments and savings. Learning this at a young age gives you the opportunity to make the changes necessary to ensure that you will not be another statistic. You will be able to put away enough money to meet your retirement financial goals.

Approximately what percentage of your income do you need to save to have a good start at saving for retirement?

A. 0 %
B. 50%
C. 25%
D. 10%
E. 75%

The answer is D, 10%. If you are in your 20s or early 30s, you should be saving at least 10% of your annual income. If you earn $30,000 a year, that's only $3,000 a year or $58 a week or $8 a day.

Approximately what percentage of your income do you need to save to catch up and have a chance for enough at retirement if you are already 45 or 50?

A. 0%
B. 50%
C. 25%
D. 10%
E. 75%

The answer is C, 25%. If you waited until your mid to upper 40s to start saving for retirement you are going to have a much tougher time. You will have to more than double the amount you would have had to save in your 20s to make up for lost time and lost interest earnings. If you earn $30,000 a year, you will have to save at least $7,500 a year, or $145 a week or $20 a day. Quite a difference!

... begin saving now for the money you will need for retirement.

Compounding

Compounding is a wonderful mathematical phenomenon. It is so powerful, that it almost seems magical. Here's how it works:

When you save or invest money, you hope to make money or get a positive rate of return. Let's say you earn 5% interest on $100 (or $5). Instead of taking the $5 out of the account, you leave it there or ***reinvest*** the $5 with the $100. Then you earn 5% on the new amount $105. This time you earn $5.25 and you reinvest that so now you have $110.25. You keep doing this and over time you are earning money on the money you earned in addition to the money you started with. This is known as COMPOUNDING.

Compounding has a snowball effect. Over time, the starting amount (in this case $100) grows faster and faster because of all the earnings that your money is making and you are reinvesting (put back into the account). Soon you are earning more money than what you even started with originally. Even if you stop

Notes:

... Student A.

... Student B.

adding new money to the account and just keep reinvesting the earnings, the amount will grow. This is how you put your money to work for you.

Look at this example:

Student A
Starts saving at age 21 and puts $2,000 a year into an investment earning 8% a year. She stops saving after 10 years and retires at age 67.

Student B
Doesn't start saving until age 35 but when she starts, she saves $2,000 a year into an investment earning 8% a year. She saves for 30 years until she retires at age 67.

Who has more money at age 67, Student A or Student B?

Student A!!!!!

Student A has approximately $500,000 after saving $20,000
Student B has approximately $250,000 after saving $60,000

Even though Student B saved more money (3 times the amount of Student A), over the 30-year period, Student A still has more money because of the power of compounding. Amazing isn't it! Hopefully this little illustration is enough to convince you to start saving, even a little, **NOW!!!!!**

Inflation

Inflation is compounding's ugly twin sister! The same way compounding seems magical, so is inflation but in a negative way.

Inflation occurs when the price for goods rises. It costs more to pay for something than it did the year before. Another way of saying it is that you can't buy as much with a dollar as you used to.

Example:

In the 1980's it cost less than $1.00 for a gallon of gas. Now it costs more than double that amount.

That's inflation.

The inflation rate, or the rate at which prices change, varies year-to-year, decade-to-decade. During the 1980's, inflation was as high as 8%. During the early part of the 2000's, inflation was in the 3% range.

Inflation is an important factor when planning for retirement. You have to plan for what costs will be when you retire since they are going to be higher and your income is going to be lower. Many people forget this and end up not saving enough. A retirement specialist can help you better understand these issues and advise you on how to proceed.

Where to Save for Retirement

401k and 403b Retirement Plans.

401k Retirement Plans are usually offered by non-governmental, private employers.

403b Retirement Plans are usually offered when you work for a school, governmental or non-profit organization.

Hopefully you have a job and your employer offers a 401k or 403b plan. If so, you should enroll in the plan as soon as you are eligible. Sometimes you have to wait one month, six months or even one year before you are allowed to sign up.

What is this 401k or 403b plan anyway?

These are retirement plans that your employer may sponsor to allow you to save money on a pre-tax basis **for retirement**. Pre-tax means the amount you put into savings is taken off your gross income before you are taxed. This lowers the amount of tax you have to pay while helping you save for retirement. This is a double win for you.

401k and 403b plans have some other benefits and lmitations you should know about:

1. **The money grows tax deferred**. This means you do not pay tax on the money you earn in these accounts until you withdraw it (take it out) which helps the money to grow faster through compounding.
2. **A company match** may be provided by your employer. If your company offers a company match, they will add money to your account up to a certain percentage. This is in addition to your regular pay (more money for you!). You can only get the match if you contribute a minimum amount so **no matter what**, if your employer offers it, **you must** contribute **at least the minimum** (in most cases 3-5% of your salary).
3. **Penalties are applied** if you take money out of the account before you are 59 ½. Remember, this is supposed to be a **retirement** account. In return for letting the money grow tax-deferred, the government will make you pay a penalty if you take the money out before 59½. You will also have to pay taxes on the money you and your employer contributed as well as on the growth on the amount you take out before retirement.

Notes:

4. **Loans are allowed** so if you *really* need to get some of this money out, you can take a loan on it but you have to pay it back with interest.
5. **Taxes are paid** on all money withdrawn from your 401k or 403b plan **at retirement**. This is because it was all contributed on a before-tax basis and you did not pay tax on any of it yet. Note: some plan administrators are starting after-tax 401k plans so you may not have to pay tax on all of it at retirement. You need to understand the type of plan offered by your employer when you enroll.
6. **There is a maximum amount you can contribute**. Currently, the maximum amount is $15,500 a year if you are under age 50 and $20,500 a year if you are 50 and over. If you can save $15,500 a year, you are way ahead of the retirement savings game.

Individual Retirement Account (IRA)

If your employer does not offer a 401k or 403b plan or you are only working part-time or you are simply not eligible, you can start an IRA. There are two types of IRA accounts, Traditional and Roth.

Traditional Ira (Tax-Deductible)

Right now we will talk about a tax-deductible IRA. This means that you can deduct the money you contribute into your IRA from your gross income. You will pay less income tax while you are working when you have a tax-deductible, Traditional IRA.

1. The current contribution has been approximately $5,000 a year if you are under age 50, but will change over time. You must check the current maximum limits each year.
2. The money grows tax-deferred
3. You pay tax on all the money when it is withdrawn because you took the tax deduction when you contributed it
4. You cannot borrow from it
5. There are penalties for taking it out before age 59½, however there are some exceptions such as buying your first house and for medical emergencies
6. If your income is over a certain limit, you may not be able to contribute to a tax-deductible Traditional IRA, or you may only be able to contribute a reduced amount.

Roth Ira

Unlike the traditional IRA, the Roth IRA is not tax deductible and does not reduce your tax rate while you are earning your income. However, some people prefer a Roth IRA for a number of reasons.

1. The current contribution has been approximately $5,000 a year if you are under 50, but will change over time. You must check the current maximum limits each year.
2. You contribute money after-tax so that when you withdraw the money, you do not pay taxes on the amount you contributed. This has a tremendous amount of appeal to people who want to keep their taxes lower **when they retire**.
3. You can take money you put in out of the Roth IRA without penalty after 5 years and for certain reasons such as paying for college, buying a house or medical emergency.
4. At retirement you do not have to pay taxes on the interest you earned on your money, or on the money you already contributed. This is a big tax savings.
5. The money grows tax-deferred.
6. If your income is higher than a certain limit, you may not be able to contribute.
7. If your income is over a certain limit, you may not be able to contribute to a Roth IRA.

Social Security

This is a Federal program that was never intended to be the sole or primary means of supporting senior citizens throughout their retirement. Social Security provides many more resources to American Citizens than just retirement funding. It also provides payments to people who are disabled, to families and children when an income provider dies and other resources as well.

As the population and demographics of our nation has shifted over the years, we see that the largest population is quickly becoming the senior community. This has serious consequences for the younger generations and for those preparing to retire. The senior population will be depending on the social security contributions of the younger generation. In addition, people are living longer and need to collect for longer periods of time. Some believe the fund is being depleted rapidly and therefore the government is working to come up with ways to fix the dilemma.

Many people are concerned that Social Security resources will either be cut or eliminated by the time they retire. It is unlikely that Social Security will totally go away but it is probable that the program will undergo massive changes by the time our youngest generations are ready to retire. That means you!

Notes:

Smart Money Tips

The lesson here is to make sure you prepare early and start saving to fund your own retirement so you are not dependent on Social Security (view it as a bonus, not as an entitlement that you count on).

- ❐ The largest amount of income is expected to come from your savings or investments.
- ❐ Social Security benefits may be reduced so don't count on receiving 100% of the benefit you are estimating. After you initially qualify for social security, the Federal Government sends you a notice detailing your benefit calculations. Consider the possibility that the amount pictured may not be the actual amount you receive.
- ❐ Most employers do not provide pension plans and you will have to save the money yourself.
- ❐ 401k and 403b plans are likely to hold most of the retirement assets you have accumulated for retirement.
- ❐ The earlier you start saving, the easier it will be to accumulate the amount that you will need for retirement.

Start saving now even if it is only $1 a day!

12

My Financial Success Story

Notes:

Back to the Future

This is the beginning of your financial future. You have set forth on a journey filled with excitement, success and contentment. On the other hand, you may also make decisions that lead you down the path of poor choices, debt and unhappiness. Now that you have the knowledge and tools, it's time to write your personal financial success story.

To help you get started consider the following quotes about money and success.

After a visit to the beach, it's hard to believe that we live in a material world.
~Pam Shaw

The real measure of your wealth is how much you'd be worth if you lost all your money.
~Author Unknown

No matter how hard you hug your money, it never hugs back.
~Quoted in P.S. I Love You, compiled by H. Jackson Brown, Jr.

Waste your money and you're only out of money, but waste your time and you've lost a part of your life.
~Michael Leboeuf

Don't aim for success if you want it; just do what you love and believe in, and it will come naturally.
~David Frost

Success: To laugh often and much, to win the respect of intelligent people and the affection of children, to earn the appreciation of honest critics and endure the betrayal of false friends, to appreciate beauty, to find the best in others, to leave the world a bit better, whether by a healthy child, a garden patch, or a redeemed social condition; to know even one life has breathed easier because you have lived. This is to have succeeded!
~Ralph Waldo Emerson

Something in human nature causes us to start slacking off at our moment of greatest accomplishment. As you become successful, you will need a great deal of self-discipline not to lose your sense of balance, humility, and commitment.
~Ross Perot

The closer one gets to the top, the more one finds there is no "top."
~Nancy Barcus

There is only one success - to be able to spend your life in your own way.
~Christopher Morley

Success is getting what you want; happiness is wanting what you get.
~Author Unknown

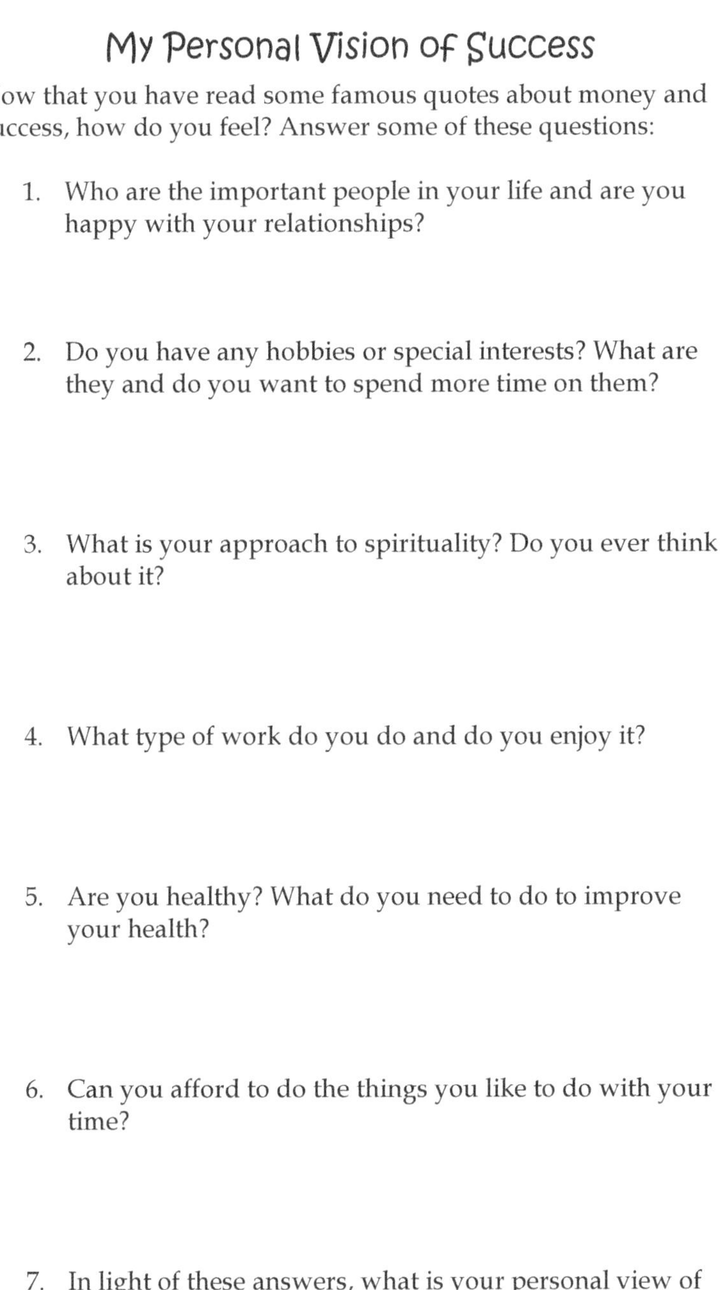

My Personal Vision of Success

Now that you have read some famous quotes about money and success, how do you feel? Answer some of these questions:

1. Who are the important people in your life and are you happy with your relationships?

2. Do you have any hobbies or special interests? What are they and do you want to spend more time on them?

3. What is your approach to spirituality? Do you ever think about it?

4. What type of work do you do and do you enjoy it?

5. Are you healthy? What do you need to do to improve your health?

6. Can you afford to do the things you like to do with your time?

7. In light of these answers, what is your personal view of success?

Notes:

My Future

Write a story that describes what your future looks like. Include things like where you want to live, what you want to do with your time, who you want to spend your time with, how you would spend your money. Use this page to write it down. Think about what would have to change in your current life situation to make your future happen the way you have written it down.

Goal Setting

By now you have realized that you do need to have goals. See what these people had to say about the importance of goals:

Goals are dreams with deadlines.
~Diana Scharf Hunt

Only those who will risk going too far can possibly find out how far one can go.
~T.S. Eliot

Map out your future, but do it in pencil.
~Jon Bon Jovi, quoted in Reader's Digest, "Quotable Quotes," September 2002

Arriving at one goal is the starting point to another.
~John Dewey

The young do not know enough to be prudent, and therefore they attempt the impossible - and achieve it, generation after generation.
~Pearl S. Buck

Smart Goals

In case you haven't already heard this, your goals should be SMART!

Specific	Write down your goal clearly and concisely
Measurable	Keep track of your progress
Attainable	Be realistic and set goals that are challenging but reachable
Rewarding	You must be able to benefit in some way from achieving the goal
Timely	Deadlines are necessary to prevent procrastination

List 3 Goals using the SMART approach that will help you achieve personal success

1.____

____

____

____

Notes:

... what is your plan for future success?

2.____

3.____

My Plan

You now have a vision of success, an idea of how you want to live your life, and a few goals that you have identified. Now you need a plan. It doesn't have to be elaborate or long. It just needs to be something that you can use as a roadmap to follow along the way. You should check it regularly to make sure you haven't gotten lost. Or maybe you will want to change the destinations and go a different route. But to get started, you need a plan. Fill in Steps 3 through 9.

Step 1 – Write your plan

Step 2 – Finish School

Step 3 – ____

Step 4 – ____

Step 5 – ______________________________

____

____

Step 6 – ______________________________

____

____

Step 7 – ______________________________

____

____

Step 8 – ______________________________

____

____

Step 9 – ______________________________

____

____

Step 10 – Review the plan at least twice a year.

Good Luck!

Notes:

Glossary

Key Terms To Understand

- ❑ **Accrued Interest** - Interest that accumulates on the unpaid principal balance of a loan.

- ❑ **Amortization -** The process of gradually paying off a loan over time through scheduled payments of principal and interest.

- ❑ **Assets -** An item of value, such as a home, business, farm, real estate, stocks, bonds, mutual funds, cash, certificates of deposit, bank accounts, trust funds and other property and investments.

- ❑ **Budget** – A detailed schedule of financial activity such as housing expenses, food, insurance costs, entertainment activity.

- ❑ **Co-insurance - A** percentage of each claim above the deductible paid by the policyholder. For a 20% health insurance coinsurance clause, the policyholder pays for the deductible plus 20% of his covered losses. After paying 80% of losses up to a specified ceiling, the insurer starts paying 100% of losses.

- ❑ **Compounding** - The process of accumulating the time value of money forward in time. For example, interest earned in one period earns additional interest during each subsequent time period.

- ❑ **Comprehensive Insurance** - Auto insurance coverage providing protection in the event of physical damage (other than collision) or theft of the insured car. For example, fire damage or a cracked windshield could be covered under the comprehensive section.

- ❑ **Consolidation -** A loan that combines several student loans into one bigger loan from a single lender. The consolidation loan is used to pay off the balances on the other loans.

- ❑ **Co-payment** - A predetermined, flat fee an individual pays for health-care services, in addition to what insurance covers. For example, some HMOs require a $10 co-payment for each office visit, regardless of the type or level of services provided during the visit. Co-payments are not usually specified by percentages.

- **Credit report** - Information communicated by a credit reporting agency that bears on a consumer's credit standing. Most credit reports include: consumer name, address, credit history, inquiries, collection records, and any public records such as bankruptcy filings and tax liens.

- **Credit score** - This term is often used to refer to credit bureau risk scores. It broadly refers to a number generated by a statistical model which is used to objectively evaluate information that pertains to making a credit decision.

- **Deductible-** Amount of loss that the insured pays before the insurance kicks in.

- **Deduction -** An expense that is allowable as a reduction of gross taxable income by the IRS (e.g., charity donations).

- **Default -** A loan is in default when the borrower fails to pay several regular installments on time (i.e., payments overdue by 270 days) or otherwise fails to meet the terms and conditions of the loan. If you default on a loan, the university, the holder of the loan, the state, and the federal government can take legal action to recovery the money, including garnishing your wages and withholding income tax refunds. Defaulting on a government loan will make you ineligible for future federal financial aid, unless a satisfactory repayment schedule is arranged, and can affect your credit rating.

- **Deferment -** Occurs when a borrower is allowed to postpone repaying the loan. If you have a subsidized loan, the federal government pays the interest charges during the deferment period. If you have an unsubsidized loan, you are responsible for the interest that accrues during the deferment period. You can still postpone paying the interest charges by capitalizing the interest, which increases the size of the loan.

  Most federal loan programs allow students to defer their loans while they are in school at least half time. If you don't qualify for a deferment, you may be able to get a forbearance. You can't get a deferment if your loan is in default.

- **Deficit -** An excess of liabilities over assets, of losses over profits, or of expenditure over income.

- **Dividends -** A portion of a company's profit paid to common and preferred shareholders. Example, a stock selling for $20 a share with an annual dividend of $1 a share yields the investor 5%.

- ❑ **Elimination Period -** The time which must pass after filing a claim before policyholder can collect insurance benefits. Also known as "waiting period."

- ❑ **Emancipated -** To release a child from the control of a parent or guardian. Declaring a child to be legally emancipated is not sufficient to release the parents or legal guardians from being responsible for providing for the child's education. The criteria for a child to be found independent are much more strict.

- ❑ **Fellowship** - A form of aid given to graduate students to help support their education. Some fellowships include a tuition waiver or a payment to the university in lieu of tuition. Most fellowships include a stipend to cover reasonable living expenses (e.g., just above the poverty line). Fellowships are a form of gift aid and do not have to be repaid.

- ❑ **FICO® scores -** Credit bureau risk scores produced from models developed by Fair Isaac Corporation are commonly known as FICO scores. Fair Isaac credit bureau scores are used by lenders and others to assess the credit risk of prospective borrowers or existing customers, in order to help make credit and marketing decisions. These scores are derived solely from the information available on credit bureau reports.

- ❑ **Gains -** A profit on a securities transaction recognized by selling a security for more than the security originally cost. The gain is the difference between the cost and the sale.

- ❑ **Grace Period** - A short time period after graduation during which the borrower is not required to begin repaying his or her student loans. The grace period may also kick in if the borrower leaves school for a reason other than graduation or drops below half-time enrollment. Depending on the type of loan, you will have a grace period of six months (Stafford Loans) or nine months (Perkins Loans) before you must start making payments on your student loans. The PLUS Loans do not have a grace period.

- ❑ **HMO Health Maintenance Organization -** Prepaid group health insurance plan that entitles members to services of participating physicians, hospitals and clinics. Emphasis is on preventative medicine, and members must use contracted health-care providers.

- ❑ **HSA Health Savings Account** - Plan that allows you to contribute pre-tax money to be used for qualified medical expenses. HSAs, which are portable, must be linked to a high-deductible health insurance policy.

- ❑ **Inflation** - The rate at which the general level of prices for goods and services is rising.

- ❑ **Interest** - The price paid for borrowing money. It is expressed as a percentage rate over a period of time such as 6 months or 12 months.

- ❑ **Liability** - A financial obligation, or outlay that must be paid back or made at a specific time to satisfy the contractual terms of such an obligation.

- ❑ **Liability Insurance** - Insurance that pays and renders service on behalf of an insured for loss arising out of his responsibility, due to negligence, to others imposed by law or assumed by contract.

- ❑ **Mutual Funds** - Mutual funds are pools of money that are managed by an investment company and regulated by the Investment Company Act of 1940. They offer investors a variety of goals, depending on the fund and its investment charter. Some funds seek to generate income on a regular basis. Others seek to preserve an investor's money. Still others seek to invest in companies that are growing at a rapid pace. Funds can impose a sales charge, or load, on investors when they buy or sell shares. No-load funds impose no sales charge.

- ❑ **Need-Based** - Financial aid that is need-based depends on your financial situation. Most government sources of financial aid are need-based.

- ❑ **Net Worth** - What you own (assets) minus what you owe (liabilities).

- ❑ **POS Point-of-Service Plan** - Health insurance policy that allows the employee to choose between in-network and out-of-network care each time medical treatment is needed.

- ❑ **PPO Preferred Provider Organization** - Network of medical providers who charge on a fee-for-service basis, but are paid on a negotiated, discounted fee schedule.

- ❑ **Pre-Existing Condition** - A coverage limitation included in many health policies which states that certain physical or mental conditions, either previously diagnosed or which would normally be expected to require treatment prior to issue, will not be covered under the new policy for a specified period of time, if at all.

- ❑ **Rate of Return** - Calculated as the (value now minus value at time of purchase) divided by value at time of purchase. Rate of return is calculated on a monthly basis, we sometimes multiply this by 12 to express an annual rate of return. This is often called the annual percentage rate (APR).

- ❑ **Simple Interest** - Interest that is paid only on the principal balance of the loan and not on any accrued interest. Most federal student loan programs offer simple interest. Note, however, that capitalizing that interest on an unsubsidized Stafford loan is a form of compounded interest.

- ❑ **Subsidized Loans** - With a subsidized loan, such as the Perkins Loan or the subsidized Stafford Loan, the government pays the interest on the loan while the student is in school, during the six-month grace period, and during any deferment periods. Subsidized loans are awarded based on financial need and may not be used to finance the family contribution.

- ❑ **Surplus -** The amount by which assets exceed liabilities.

- ❑ **Tax Deductible -** The effect of creating a tax deduction, such as charitable contributions and mortgage interest.

- ❑ **Tax Deferred -** Allowing the capital gains tax on an asset to be payable only when the gain is realized by selling the asset.

- ❑ **UGMA - Uniform Gifts to Minors Act**
  Legislation that provides a tax-effective manner of transferring property to minors without the complications of trusts or guardianship restrictions.

- ❑ **UTMA - Uniform Transfers to Minors Act**
  A law similar to the Uniform Gifts to Minors Act that extends the definition of gifts to include real estate, paintings, royalties, and patents.

- ❑ **Underwriting** - The process of selecting risks for insurance and classifying them according to their degrees of insurability so that the appropriate rates may be assigned. The process also includes rejection of those risks that do not qualify.

- ❑ **Unsubsidized loans -** A loan for which the government does not pay the interest. The borrower is responsible for the interest on an unsubsidized loan from the date the loan is disbursed, even while the student is still in school. Students may avoid paying the interest while they are in school by capitalizing the interest, which increases the loan amount. Unsubsidized loans are not based on financial need and may be used to finance the family contribution.

- **Variable Interest** - In a variable interest loan, the interest rate changes periodically. For example, the interest rate might be pegged to the cost of US Treasury Bills (e.g., T-Bill rate plus 3.1%) and be updated monthly, quarterly, semi-annually or annually.

Appendix

Form W-4 (2009)

Purpose. Complete Form W-4 so that your employer can withhold the correct federal income tax from your pay. Consider completing a new Form W-4 each year and when your personal or financial situation changes.

Exemption from withholding. If you are exempt, complete **only** lines 1, 2, 3, 4, and 7 and sign the form to validate it. Your exemption for 2009 expires February 16, 2010. See Pub. 505, Tax Withholding and Estimated Tax.

Note. You cannot claim exemption from withholding if (a) your income exceeds $950 and includes more than $300 of unearned income (for example, interest and dividends) and (b) another person can claim you as a dependent on their tax return.

Basic instructions. If you are not exempt, complete the **Personal Allowances Worksheet** below. The worksheets on page 2 further adjust your withholding allowances based on itemized deductions, certain credits, adjustments to income, or two-earner/multiple job situations.

Complete all worksheets that apply. However, you may claim fewer (or zero) allowances. For regular wages, withholding must be based on allowances you claimed and may not be a flat amount or percentage of wages.

Head of household. Generally, you may claim head of household filing status on your tax return only if you are unmarried and pay more than 50% of the costs of keeping up a home for yourself and your dependent(s) or other qualifying individuals. See Pub. 501, Exemptions, Standard Deduction, and Filing Information, for information.

Tax credits. You can take projected tax credits into account in figuring your allowable number of withholding allowances. Credits for child or dependent care expenses and the child tax credit may be claimed using the **Personal Allowances Worksheet** below. See Pub. 919, How Do I Adjust My Tax Withholding, for information on converting your other credits into withholding allowances.

Nonwage income. If you have a large amount of nonwage income, such as interest or dividends, consider making estimated tax payments using Form 1040-ES, Estimated Tax for Individuals. Otherwise, you may owe additional tax. If you have pension or annuity income, see Pub. 919 to find out if you should adjust your withholding on Form W-4 or W-4P.

Two earners or multiple jobs. If you have a working spouse or more than one job, figure the total number of allowances you are entitled to claim on all jobs using worksheets from only one Form W-4. Your withholding usually will be most accurate when all allowances are claimed on the Form W-4 for the highest paying job and zero allowances are claimed on the others. See Pub. 919 for details.

Nonresident alien. If you are a nonresident alien, see the Instructions for Form 8233 before completing this Form W-4.

Check your withholding. After your Form W-4 takes effect, use Pub. 919 to see how the amount you are having withheld compares to your projected total tax for 2009. See Pub. 919, especially if your earnings exceed $130,000 (Single) or $180,000 (Married).

Personal Allowances Worksheet (Keep for your records.)

A Enter "1" for **yourself** if no one else can claim you as a dependent . . . . **A** ______

B Enter "1" if:
- You are single and have only one job; or
- You are married, have only one job, and your spouse does not work; or
- Your wages from a second job or your spouse's wages (or the total of both) are $1,500 or less.

. . **B** ______

C Enter "1" for your **spouse.** But, you may choose to enter "-0-" if you are married and have either a working spouse or more than one job. (Entering "-0-" may help you avoid having too little tax withheld.) . . . . **C** ______

D Enter number of **dependents** (other than your spouse or yourself) you will claim on your tax return . . . . . . **D** ______

E Enter "1" if you will file as **head of household** on your tax return (see conditions under **Head of household** above) . **E** ______

F Enter "1" if you have at least $1,800 of **child or dependent care expenses** for which you plan to claim a credit . . **F** ______
(**Note.** Do **not** include child support payments. See Pub. 503, Child and Dependent Care Expenses, for details.)

G **Child Tax Credit** (including additional child tax credit). See Pub. 972, Child Tax Credit, for more information.
- If your total income will be less than $61,000 ($90,000 if married), enter "2" for each eligible child; then **less** "1" if you have three or more eligible children.
- If your total income will be between $61,000 and $84,000 ($90,000 and $119,000 if married), enter "1" for each eligible child plus "1" **additional** if you have six or more eligible children. **G** ______

H Add lines A through G and enter total here. (**Note.** This may be different from the number of exemptions you claim on your tax return.) ▶ **H** ______

For accuracy, **complete all worksheets that apply.**
- If you plan to **itemize or claim adjustments to income** and want to reduce your withholding, see the **Deductions and Adjustments Worksheet** on page 2.
- If you have **more than one job** or are **married and you and your spouse both work** and the combined earnings from all jobs exceed $40,000 ($25,000 if married), see the **Two-Earners/Multiple Jobs Worksheet** on page 2 to avoid having too little tax withheld.
- If **neither** of the above situations applies, **stop here** and enter the number from line H on line 5 of Form W-4 below.

Cut here and give Form W-4 to your employer. Keep the top part for your records.

Form **W-4**
Department of the Treasury
Internal Revenue Service

Employee's Withholding Allowance Certificate

▶ **Whether you are entitled to claim a certain number of allowances or exemption from withholding is subject to review by the IRS. Your employer may be required to send a copy of this form to the IRS.**

OMB No. 1545-0074
2009

1 Type or print your first name and middle initial.	Last name	2 **Your social security number**
Home address (number and street or rural route)	3 ☐ Single ☐ Married ☐ Married, but withhold at higher Single rate. **Note.** If married, but legally separated, or spouse is a nonresident alien, check the "Single" box.	
City or town, state, and ZIP code	4 **If your last name differs from that shown on your social security card, check here. You must call 1-800-772-1213 for a replacement card.** ▶ ☐	

5 Total number of allowances you are claiming (from line **H** above **or** from the applicable worksheet on page 2) **5** ______

6 Additional amount, if any, you want withheld from each paycheck . . . . **6** $ ______

7 I claim exemption from withholding for 2009, and I certify that I meet **both** of the following conditions for exemption.
- Last year I had a right to a refund of **all** federal income tax withheld because I had **no** tax liability **and**
- This year I expect a refund of **all** federal income tax withheld because I expect to have **no** tax liability.

If you meet both conditions, write "Exempt" here . . . . ▶ **7** ______

Under penalties of perjury, I declare that I have examined this certificate and to the best of my knowledge and belief, it is true, correct, and complete.

Employee's signature
(Form is not valid unless you sign it.) ▶ **Date** ▶

8 Employer's name and address (Employer: Complete lines 8 and 10 only if sending to the IRS.)	**9** Office code (optional)	**10** Employer identification number (EIN)

For Privacy Act and Paperwork Reduction Act Notice, see page 2. Cat. No. 10220Q Form **W-4** (2009)

Deductions and Adjustments Worksheet

Note. Use this worksheet *only* if you plan to itemize deductions, claim certain credits, adjustments to income, or an additional standard deduction.

1 Enter an estimate of your 2009 itemized deductions. These include qualifying home mortgage interest, charitable contributions, state and local taxes, medical expenses in excess of 7.5% of your income, and miscellaneous deductions. (For 2009, you may have to reduce your itemized deductions if your income is over $166,800 ($83,400 if married filing separately). See *Worksheet 2* in Pub. 919 for details.) . . 1 $________

2 Enter: { $11,400 if married filing jointly or qualifying widow(er); $ 8,350 if head of household; $ 5,700 if single or married filing separately } . . . . 2 $________

3 **Subtract** line 2 from line 1. If zero or less, enter "-0-" . . . . 3 $________

4 Enter an estimate of your 2009 adjustments to income and any additional standard deduction. (Pub. 919) . . . . 4 $________

5 **Add** lines 3 and 4 and enter the total. (Include any amount for credits from *Worksheet 8* in Pub. 919.) . 5 $________

6 Enter an estimate of your 2009 nonwage income (such as dividends or interest) . . . . 6 $________

7 **Subtract** line 6 from line 5. If zero or less, enter "-0-" . . . . 7 $________

8 **Divide** the amount on line 7 by $3,500 and enter the result here. Drop any fraction . . . . 8 ________

9 Enter the number from the **Personal Allowances Worksheet,** line H, page 1 . . . . 9 ________

10 **Add** lines 8 and 9 and enter the total here. If you plan to use the **Two-Earners/Multiple Jobs Worksheet,** also enter this total on line 1 below. Otherwise, **stop here** and enter this total on Form W-4, line 5, page 1 10 ________

Two-Earners/Multiple Jobs Worksheet (See *Two earners or multiple jobs* on page 1.)

Note. Use this worksheet *only* if the instructions under line H on page 1 direct you here.

1 Enter the number from line H, page 1 (or from line 10 above if you used the **Deductions and Adjustments Worksheet**) 1 ________

2 Find the number in **Table 1** below that applies to the **LOWEST** paying job and enter it here. **However,** if you are married filing jointly and wages from the highest paying job are $50,000 or less, do not enter more than "3." . . . . 2 ________

3 If line 1 is **more than or equal to** line 2, subtract line 2 from line 1. Enter the result here (if zero, enter "-0-") and on Form W-4, line 5, page 1. **Do not** use the rest of this worksheet . . . . 3 ________

Note. If line 1 is *less than* line 2, enter "-0-" on Form W-4, line 5, page 1. Complete lines 4–9 below to calculate the additional withholding amount necessary to avoid a year-end tax bill.

4 Enter the number from line 2 of this worksheet . . . . 4 ________

5 Enter the number from line 1 of this worksheet . . . . 5 ________

6 **Subtract** line 5 from line 4 . . . . 6 ________

7 Find the amount in **Table 2** below that applies to the **HIGHEST** paying job and enter it here . . . . 7 $________

8 **Multiply** line 7 by line 6 and enter the result here. This is the additional annual withholding needed . . 8 $________

9 Divide line 8 by the number of pay periods remaining in 2009. For example, divide by 26 if you are paid every two weeks and you complete this form in December 2008. Enter the result here and on Form W-4, line 6, page 1. This is the additional amount to be withheld from each paycheck . . . . 9 $

Table 1

Married Filing Jointly		All Others	
If wages from **LOWEST** paying job are—	Enter on line 2 above	If wages from **LOWEST** paying job are—	Enter on line 2 above
$0 - $4,500	0	$0 - $6,000	0
4,501 - 9,000	1	6,001 - 12,000	1
9,001 - 18,000	2	12,001 - 19,000	2
18,001 - 22,000	3	19,001 - 26,000	3
22,001 - 26,000	4	26,001 - 35,000	4
26,001 - 32,000	5	35,001 - 50,000	5
32,001 - 38,000	6	50,001 - 65,000	6
38,001 - 46,000	7	65,001 - 80,000	7
46,001 - 55,000	8	80,001 - 90,000	8
55,001 - 60,000	9	90,001 - 120,000	9
60,001 - 65,000	10	120,001 and over	10
65,001 - 75,000	11		
75,001 - 95,000	12		
95,001 - 105,000	13		
105,001 - 120,000	14		
120,001 and over	15		

Table 2

Married Filing Jointly		All Others	
If wages from **HIGHEST** paying job are—	Enter on line 7 above	If wages from **HIGHEST** paying job are—	Enter on line 7 above
$0 - $65,000	$550	$0 - $35,000	$550
65,001 - 120,000	910	35,001 - 90,000	910
120,001 - 185,000	1,020	90,001 - 165,000	1,020
185,001 - 330,000	1,200	165,001 - 370,000	1,200
330,001 and over	1,280	370,001 and over	1,280

Privacy Act and Paperwork Reduction Act Notice. We ask for the information on this form to carry out the Internal Revenue laws of the United States. The Internal Revenue Code requires this information under sections 3402(f)(2)(A) and 6109 and their regulations. Failure to provide a properly completed form will result in your being treated as a single person who claims no withholding allowances; providing fraudulent information may also subject you to penalties. Routine uses of this information include giving it to the Department of Justice for civil and criminal litigation, to cities, states, the District of Columbia, and U.S. commonwealths and possessions for use in administering their tax laws, and using it in the National Directory of New Hires. We may also disclose this information to other countries under a tax treaty, to federal and state agencies to enforce federal nontax criminal laws, or to federal law enforcement and intelligence agencies to combat terrorism.

You are not required to provide the information requested on a form that is subject to the Paperwork Reduction Act unless the form displays a valid OMB control number. Books or records relating to a form or its instructions must be retained as long as their contents may become material in the administration of any Internal Revenue law. Generally, tax returns and return information are confidential, as required by Code section 6103.

The average time and expenses required to complete and file this form will vary depending on individual circumstances. For estimated averages, see the instructions for your income tax return.

If you have suggestions for making this form simpler, we would be happy to hear from you. See the instructions for your income tax return.

Asset Allocation

Asset allocation is an investment strategy that spreads your investment across various types of investments, such as stocks and bonds. (*Asset allocation does not assure a profit or protect against loss in a declining market.*) The unpredictable ups and downs of the financial markets are a constant reminder of the critical role of proper asset allocation and diversification.

Important Considerations

- There is no assurance that an asset allocation model will not lose money or that investment results will not experience some volatility.
- Market and asset class performance may differ in the future from the historical performance and assumptions upon which the asset allocation models are built.
- Directed Allocation Models are not guaranteed to outperform an individual fund or group of funds.
- Asset allocation model performance is dependent upon the performance of the funds in the model.
- The timing of your investment and the frequency of automatic rebalancing may affect performance.
- The value of the funds will fluctuate, and when redeemed, may be worth more or less than the original cost.
- We have the right to terminate or change the Asset Allocation Program at any time.

Investor Profile: Risk Tolerance Questionnaire

The following questions are designed to help match an investor to the most appropriate annuity asset allocation model based on answers to questions about an individual's time horizon and risk tolerance.

Circle the letter (a, b, c, d or e) next to your answers, then refer to the scoring information following this questionnaire to determine your recommended asset allocation model.

Risk Capacity

1. Year age

a. Over 65
b. 60 to 65
c. 55 to 59
d. 50 to 54
e. Under 50

2. Within the next six years, how confident are you that you will have sufficient liquidity to meet your ongoing expenses and any predictable financial obligations (e.g. mortgages, college expenses or dependent care services etc.)?

a. not confident, unsure, or really don't know
b. somewhat confident
c. confident
d. very confident
e. completely confident

3. Which statement best describes your experience investing in equity markets?

a. I have not invested in stocks or mutual funds before or I am very dissatisfied with my equity investing experience; I don't understand the prospectus at all; I am uncomfortable with stock market investments; I don't know what 'risk vs. reward' means.
b. I have had a very limited investing experience or I am somewhat dissatisfied with my past equity investing experience; I find the prospectus confusing; I would prefer a more conservative investment strategy; 'risk vs. reward' makes me uncomfortable.
c. I have less than 10 years of experience investing in stocks or mutual funds; I am comfortable making some equity investments, but also want some balance with fixed income; I understand 'risk vs. reward'; I am comfortable seeking growth with fixed income.
d. I have 10-15 years experience investing in stocks or mutual funds; I carefully read the prospectus of any investment before investing; I am comfortable making equity investments; I understand 'risk vs. reward'; I am comfortable seeking greater capital appreciation with some fixed income.
e. I have more than 20 years of experience investing in stocks or mutual funds; I often refer to a prospectus or research online for investment details; I understand the idea of 'risk vs. reward,' I am confident in more aggressive investments.

Risk Attitude

4. Which best describes your attitude toward investing?

a. I cannot afford any possible loss of principal and worry a lot about market declines.

b. I prefer to have my entire portfolio invested in lower-risk equity and fixed income assets, with less volatility and lower capital risk (typically, with lower returns).

c. I like to have a broadly-balanced portfolio consisting of high-, medium- and low-risk investments, in a well diversified mix of asset classes.

d. I seek mostly investments with a likely potential for high growth, with a minor stake in fixed income investments, tolerating market fluctuations without great concern.

a. I want higher returns, and will accept greater market volatility (and possibly, major setbacks), to try to achieve that goal with more aggressive investments.

5. Hare are hypothetical returns for a $100,000 investment portfolio over a five-year investment period. Which characteristics do you find most acceptable for both reward and risk?

	Median Annual Return	Best Year	Worst Year
a.	5%	15%	-5%
b.	6%	20%	-10%
c.	7%	25%	-15% .
d.	8%	30%	-25%
e.	9%	40%	-30%

6. Capital markets have always experienced significant price swings (rising and falling value). Imagine that your investment goal is five years away, but your well-diversified portfolio loses 20% of its value in a brief period. What best describes your reaction?

a. I would abandon that investment vehicle.

b. I would immediately switch to a more conservative strategy.

c. I would not wait until the year-end review before reorganizing my portfolio.

d. I would wait to reassess my portfolio at year-end review before making any big changes.

e. I would not alter my portfolio.

7. I would describe my current investing objectives/goals as:

a. very conservative, and worried about equity investments

b. conservative, reducing exposure to market swings

c. moderate (with growth and income), or a more balanced strategy

d. growth-oriented, primarily

e. somewhat aggressive

Scoring Your Answers:

Your total score will determine the type of investor you are. Once you know that, review the two options available to you for suggestions on how to diversify your variable annuity investment.

- For Questions 1-7, assign the following points to your answer: a = 1 point, b = 2 points, c = 3 points, d = 4 points, and e = 5 points.
- Add your score for each question.

Total Score:

7-10 points
You may have identified serious investment concerns, and may require additional investment guidance and/or financial education. Equity investing may not be suitable for you.

11-15 points
Your profile confirms conservative positioning; alternately, you might still have critical financial concerns, or have strong risk aversion to the fluctuations of equity investments.

16-20 points
Your profile indicates you may be inclined toward a balanced style of investing, with conservative attributes.

21-25 points
Your profile indicates you may be inclined toward a moderate growth style of investing, with a fairly secure outlook.

26-30 points
Your profile indicates you may be seeking a portfolio with solid capital appreciation potential and relatively more risk (a growth style of investing).

31-35 points
Your profile indicates you may be geared toward an aggressive portfolio with strong capital appreciation potential and greater risk.

Important Resources

www CollegeBoard.com

This is a great not-for-profit organization that offers you information about college preparation including determining which college or career is good for you, how to apply, where to get loans, tests you need to take such as SATs, college costs, and much, much more.

www.myFICO.com

The Fair Isaac Corporation website that provides great information on credit scores. Basically everything you need to know including how to order your credit report and understand how to read it.

www.FinAid.com

FinAid.com is a comprehensive source of financial aid information. This is probably one of the best one-stop resources for this type of information.

www.studentloans.com

This is a not-for-profit organization that helps students and their parents get information about all different types of loans such as Stafford, PLUS and private loans from lending institutions.

www.iii.org

The Insurance Information Institute provides information about insurance and how it works. It has information on all types of insurance and also offers statistics.

www Idealist.org

For those students who want to volunteer or provide services to communities, this website offers a wealth of information and contacts.

www.savinisbonds.gov

Provides information about Federal Savings Bonds, and you can check the value of any bonds you have. There is also a savings bond wizard site that helps you to organize and track your bonds.

www.craigslist.org

This site is an on-line classified tool. It provides links to find apartments, buy used items, find jobs, cars and even help you post a job if you need to hire someone.

www.IRS.gov

This website brings you directly to the Internal Revenue Service (IRS) Directory. You can access any tax forms you need such as the W-4 or W-2, get information about paying your taxes, and statistics about taxes.

www.AICPA.org

The American Institute of Certified Public Accountants can help you find a tax professional to help you understand some of the tax issues you will face. It also provides resources on taxes and other financial concerns.

www DOL.com

This is the official Department of Labor website. You can find information about unemployment insurance and the website for your State Department of Labor.

www.SallieMae.com

Sallie Mae is a national organization that provides information and resources about obtaining student loans and paying for college.

www.FAFSA.ed.gov

Provides all the information you need to obtain the FAFSA forms, fill them out and obtain information about other student aid.

Index

www.ingramcontent.com/pod-product-compliance
Lightning Source LLC
LaVergne TN
LVHW061223100826
845148LV00004B/845

* 9 7 8 1 5 8 1 0 7 1 5 6 6 *